Dunces With Wolves

The third volume of the Bernard Jones Diaries

by Nick Louth

To Ann

Nick Louth

Harriman House Ltd
3A Penns Road
Petersfield
Hampshire
GU32 2EW

Tel. +44 (0)1730 233870
Fax +44(0)1730 233880
Email: enquiries@harriman-house.com
Website: www.harriman-house.com

First published in Great Britain in 2008 by Harriman House Ltd.
Ludensian Books
Copyright © Nick Louth

www.nicklouth.com

www.bernardjones.co.uk

ISBN 13: 9781906659011

British Library Cataloguing in Publication Data
A CIP catalogue record for this book can be obtained from the British Library

Printed and bound by Biddles Ltd.

Praise For The Bernard Jones Diaries

"In Bernard Jones, Nick Louth has produced an anti-hero for our financial age. Whether it is fighting his way to a secure retirement, jousting with the council over wheelie bins or feuding with his wife over his fondness for cakes and biscuits, Bernard Jones goes into battle on behalf of us all."

Matthew Vincent, *Financial Times*

"Nick Louth delightfully and painfully accurately brings to life the travails of the amateur investor as he tries to make his pension stretch that little bit further. Nick's wry humour and witty focus on human relationships and frailties is a must read and requires no knowledge of finance to enjoy."

Ashley Seager, *The Guardian*

"Just as chick-lit heroine Bridget Jones struggles with men, retired anti-hero Bernard Jones is bemused by the trials and tribulations of investing. Anyone who is a member of an investment club will instantly recognise the characters in this clever, well crafted and highly amusing book."

Brian Durrant, Investment Director, The Fleet Street Letter

"Bernard Jones, tried by life, marriage, family, friends and neighbours as much as by investment is a must-read. He's on the way to becoming a minor classic."

Chris Crowcroft, *Investors Chronicle* reader

"I have found myself laughing out loud and occasionally in giggles!"

Mark Hobhouse, *Investors Chronicle* reader

"I have enjoyed reading Bernard Jones Diary as he attempts to enjoy retirement with a mixture of cunning and (not too much) knowledge. I wish him well."

Eric Cox, *Investors Chronicle* reader

"It's so easy to identify with Bernard Jones and the situations he describes. I almost feel I know him as a friend. His diary is the first page I turn to in the magazine. It is always topical and hugely entertaining."

Leonard Spark, *Investors Chronicle* reader

"Small time investor Bernard Jones juggles with middle age, a wife, a grown up family, an elderly mother, foul neighbours and investments. His only pleasures are his indulgence in secretive sweet treats and a Hornby train set. Life shifts up a gear when a pretty au pair arrives next door."

Joe Vella, *Investors Chronicle* reader

"Bernard and I are soul mates...We share the same hopeless investing traits being driven by misty eyed emotion, alcohol and a love of chocolate rather than the cold logical appraisal of information so beloved by the professionals."

Gordon Gray, New Zealand, *Investors Chronicle* reader

"A must read for the private investor...Share the highs and lows of life with Bernard as he battles the twin impostors of triumph and despair (not in equal measure unfortunately)."

Tony Watson, *Investors Chronicle* reader

"Don't miss Bernard's diary, it will brighten your day. This addictive column is so true to life."

Paul Hunt, *Investors Chronicle* reader

About The Author

Nick Louth is a financial journalist, author and investment commentator. He has regular columns in the *Financial Times*, the *Investors Chronicle* and on the MSN Money website.

His first book, an investment guide called *Multiply your Money*, was published by McGraw Hill in November 2001. The *Investment Diary of Bernard Jones* followed in February 2007 and a novel, *Bite*, in October 2007. The second volume of the Bernard Jones Diaries, *Bernard Jones and the Temple of Mammon*, was published in November 2007.

Nick Louth is married and lives in Lincolnshire.

Foreword

Bernard Jones was born as a one-off feature idea for the *Investors Chronicle* for the Christmas edition of 2005. Almost three years later *Dunces with Wolves* is the third volume of the Bernard Jones Diaries, proof, perhaps, that something begun on a whim can soon take on a life of its own.

The story of Bernard is really an attempt to dissolve the hyperbolic claims of the investment world with a dose of blunt reality. Far from regaling readers with yet another grandiose tale, such as *How I Made A Million In Forty-Eight Hours While Lying By The Pool With My Three Supermodel Girlfriends* I decided to pursue the more realistic story: *How I Lost £1283.46 In An Hour And A Quarter When I Forgot To Sell My Shares In Northern Rock Because The Header Tank In The Loft Was Leaking Into The Spare Bedroom And Ruining My Wife's Cardigan Collection.*

Bernard Jones probably spends more time up a ladder being hen-pecked about cardigans than the average investor, and certainly more time being supervised while trimming leylandii hedges than any hedge fund manager. For all the experience he has gained, either with über-successful investor and friend 'Perfect' Peter Edgington or the group of amateurs who make up the Hell's Bells share club at the Ring o'Bells pub, it hasn't done him the slightest bit of good.

Dunces with Wolves is more than a collection of previously published columns. As with the previous volumes, more than a third is new and unpublished material. That is either because some plot lines were too long for the limited space in the magazine, or in some cases too racy. I'll leave you to decide. So if you want to experience what it's like to be French kissed by a tax inspector you've got to read on, because you won't find it in back copies of the *Investors Chronicle*.[1]

---

[1] However, you will find guidance on the deductability of osculatory transactions in *The HMRC Guide To Schedule D* in the chapter entitled 'Miscellaneous Oral Exchanges' (HMSO 2003).

The first volume of the diaries, *Funny Money* was published in February 2007 by Ludensian Books. The second volume, *Bernard Jones and the Temple of Mammon*, was published in November 2007 by Harriman House.

There is much more background information on Bernard Jones and the other characters at the website www.bernardjones.co.uk and on the *Investors Chronicle* website www.investorschronicle.co.uk. The author would be pleased to receive reader's feedback at www.nicklouth.com.

Introduction

Bernard Jones is one of life's losers. The retired civil servant and amateur investor lets opportunities shoot through his fingers as easily as the last splinter of soap in a Travelodge bathroom. Frustrated by decades of marriage to the demanding Eunice, Bernard loses himself in the den at the back of the house, which he has renamed Lemon Curdistan. In this self-styled republic, he slaves over his personal computer dreaming of untold stock market riches.

Eunice, whose carnal appetites have not been blunted by advancing years or dress size, has quite different plans for her husband, which Bernard refers to under the dreaded sobriquet 'hippopotamus manoeuvres'. What Eunice fails to understand is that her husband's desires in this area shrivelled along with the pound in your pocket sometime during Harold Wilson's premiership. But Eunice is a modern woman. Together with her trendy vegan friend Irmgard and near-neighbour Daphne Hanson-Hart, she is quite open about Bernard's deficiencies whether they be pensions, passions or prostate. She is particularly determined to steer him from his preferred elevenses of biscuits and cakes towards healthier fare, preferably probiotic yoghurt, lentils and obscure Fairtrade fruit.

Despite more than six decades of life experience, Bernard's timing remains impeccably bad. He can be relied upon to miss every chance to sell a losing share before it is worthless. Even on the rare occasion that he stumbles upon a winner, you can be sure that he will hastily sell as soon as he's gained 5% and watch in impotent fury as its price then shoots into orbit.

Bernard's eccentric and addled mother, Dot, has the very fortune to which he aspires. However, the demented but determined nonagenarian is determined to keep it from him. Instead, she has turned to Mary Asterby, leader of the local Women's Institute, whose steely resolve and bookkeeping acumen is just the ticket to prevent Bernard's inheritance dissolving along with Britain's banking system.

Some of the same skill would have come in handy at The Ring o'Bells, the run-down pub in which the Hell's Bells share club meets. There, a coterie of cash-strapped investment dunces tangle with the world's financial wolves, and usually come off worse. They include Harry Staines, septuagenarian former navy officer, whose greatest ever stock pick was five unattended boxes of pork scratchings left next to the pub toilet. Then there is K.P. Sharma, successful Ugandan Asian businessman, who parlayed a successful chain of convenience stores into a disastrous shareholding in several of Britain's failing banks. Severely indebted Martin Gale remains addicted to get-rich schemes which can only make him poorer, while curry and cigarette enthusiast Mike Delaney stays with the stalwart holdings of the tobacco sector. Scrapdealer's daughter Chantelle, who carries a wide selection of ferrous metals in her many piercings, is one of the canniest members of the club as well as the youngest. But as the only woman, and the barmaid at the Ring o'Bells, she struggles to make her nous count when decisions are eventually made. If only the club's real high-flier, city banker Cynthia Valkenberg, wasn't now languishing in a U.S. jail they would know what to do.

There is no such trouble with Bernard's fiendishly brilliant grandson, Digby, a.k.a. the Antichrist. The nine-year-old, only child of Bernard's *Guardian*-reading son Brian and daughter-in-law Janet, has both computer genius and a business brain. He even looks like becoming a chess grandmaster until he comes up against 'Perfect' Peter Edgington, Bernard's former colleague and investment guru. However, the malicious child's precocious attempts to make online contact with the East European mafia end up costing Bernard a friendship.

Bernard finds some solace on an overseas trip for the Hell's Bells share club. Though what its members know about emerging markets could be written on the wrapper of a Cadbury's Creme Egg, they know cheap beer and the lure of an exotic nightlife when they see it.

However, it is when Bernard's 92-year-old mother disappears on her mobility scooter Maurice that Bernard finally realises the truth: that there is more to life than money, and more to families than securing an inheritance.

Chapter One

Scissors And Suffering

Tuesday 11th September 2007: Hair-Raising Incidents

On this day, a sombre anniversary, I am reminded that the world is beset with conflict. Real wars in Iraq and Afghanistan, simmering friction between Israel and the Palestinians. Then there are economic conflicts: inflation, the banking crisis and soaring oil prices. While yours truly struggles at his personal computer to steer the family investment portfolio between these giant fiscal storms, an even greater cloud is spreading its mushroom-shaped darkness. My wife has fallen out with her hairdresser.

The first I know of this hirsute holocaust was when Eunice burst into Lemon Curdistan, my den at the back of the house where as the lonely captain at my PC, I peer into the dark heart of the investing storm.

"Look what she's done to me, Bernard," she said, breathlessly. "Just look."

"What *who's* done to you?"

"Just look! It's an absolute disaster. We've got that reception at St Simeon's church tomorrow night. Sir Giles and Lady Topham will be there. And I simply *cannot* go like this."

I blink in disbelief, scanning my wife's matronly frame for the terminal damage that has apparently been inflicted on her.

"It's that damn Stacey at Catwalk Cuts. Look, just LOOK," she said turning around and running her hands through her hair above the back of her neck. In truth I'd expected there to be a pair of pinking shears buried in there up to the handle, perhaps a livid burn, or possibly the repeated slashes of a mishandled razor. But no, it was hair, and apart from being a bit tabby, it looked – well, it just looked like hair. You might as well have asked me whether the hairs

3

on a badger's backside should be straight or curly, black or white, or parted on the left or right. I am a man, and I therefore had literally no clue whatever as to what I should say about the hair I could see on the back of my wife's head. At least she'd got some there. Nevertheless, I knew it was imperative to agree with her before a minute was up and to do so without hesitation, deviation or delay.

"Well, I must say," I started, trying to give myself time to think. "It does look, rather like a..."

The trouble was that in my head I could now only think of one image, so lucid, so vivid and so plainly not what she wanted to hear: a badger's bum.

"It does, er, resemble," I said. Go on, say it. Badger's bum, badger's bum, badger's bum. The little self-destructive voice in myself clamoured to be heard, to shout out for all the world to hear. Badger's bum, badger's bum. Go on, Bernard, have courage. Tell her it looks like a badger's bum.

"Well, the way they've coloured it, it looks a teeny bit like a badger's bottom, doesn't it?" I said.

Eunice spun around to face me like a rocket-powered Bolshoi ballerina. "What? It's not the colour, Bernard! It hasn't *been* coloured, has it? I mean look, that's my normal colour, with the highlights, isn't it?"

"Is it? Oh, yes. So it is," I squeaked. Ah, so badger isn't a problem on the colour front. What was I to say?

"So what exactly is the problem, then?" I asked.

"Bernard. It is perfectly obvious. Stacey has cut it all wrong. I told her exactly what I wanted right at the start. Just look at it!"

"Is it a bit too short then?" Desperation, sheer desperation.

"No, no, no, Bernard. Come here." She summoned me out to the hall mirror, where she could give me a personalised audio-guided tour of the battlefield. "It's not the length, it's the *type* of cut. I'd told her I wanted it feathered. And as you can clearly see she's gone and layered it," she said, plumping and preening the badger's bum-like tufts in question.

"Ah. Has she. Ah. Well, if you're not happy, I should complain."

"I *have* complained," Eunice snorted. "And they offered me £10 off. I mean, that's ridiculous."

"Why didn't you take it? I mean that would be a virtually free cut, I imagine."

"Hardly, Bernard. I used to pay £35 for Mr Paul..."

"Thirty-five quid! For a haircut!"

"No Bernard, for a wash, conditioner, design consultation and cut. Anyway Paul, who was principal stylist, left in 2006. Since then I've had Lorraine, who is a senior stylist..."

"And how much does she charge?"

"Well, all the senior stylists went up in July to £38. But then they brought in Stacey as styling director, and I was recommended to see her because she was so highly thought of, having worked under Sebastian Montrachet in Paris."

Never heard of him. "Come on then, what's the damage?"

"Well. It's £60. So ten pounds off was hardly the point."

My jaw hung open. After decades of practice keeping my mouth shut I thought I'd already reconciled myself to the staggering expense in shoes, clothes, cosmetics and personal care products of keeping my wife slightly less unsightly in late middle age than she would otherwise be. But no. My head reeled at this largesse, ladled out fortnightly to the scissor-wielding mafia of the Home Counties.

"Good God, woman, that's over £1500 a year! That's more than our council tax! How on earth do they justify it?"

"Well, last time they went up they said it was because of the increase in minimum wage."

"Ridiculous! The minimum wage is less than six quid an hour. Do they take ten hours to do your hair? Or are there teams of a dozen, lovingly caressing each superannuated follicle in turn."

"Bernard, I'm the one who's cross, not you..."

"And all this stuff and nonsense about principal stylists and what not. Presumably, it's only a matter of time before they bring in a chief executive stylist who earns £1.2 million a year, has a company helicopter, share options and a gratis flat in the Barbican."

"Oh for goodness' sake, now you're exaggerating."

"Look, I really think you should economise. I get my hair cut for £6.50, once a month."

"Don't try that one on me, Bernard. You only go to that tawdry old barber here because he's got copies of *Men Only* and *Club International* lurking among the car and fishing magazines. The place is dirty, the floor is never swept, and it's full of labourers and van drivers. Besides," she said, peering at my thinning pate, "on a cost per hair basis £6.50 works out a great deal more expensive that Catwalk Cuts."

Wednesday 12th September: Rockslide

"Look what came in the post today," said Chantelle, as we arrived for share club at the Ring o'Bells.

She shows us an airmailed envelope marked Federal Correctional Institute of Danbury, Connecticut. Inside is a brief letter from former share club member Cynthia Valkenburg.

We knew Cynthia as a stylish City high-flier, originally from Canada, whose skills and acumen revolutionised our portfolio and its performance. However, years ago she had been a non-executive director of an Antiguan-based blackjack website serving gamblers in the U.S. and elsewhere. The American authorities had deemed that a violation of Federal Wire Acts which ban the transmission of bets, originally by telegraph, but now by implication between computers. Cynthia was arrested two months ago when changing planes in the U.S. and is now serving five years in a Federal Penitentiary, though I doubt she is all that penitent. The letter describes a prison which is all-female and low security, with decent food and a tolerable regime. If she was serving time in a state prison, she would not perhaps be so lucky.

Having extricated and repaid her dominant share of the share club portfolio, what is left is looking in a very sorry state. True, our shares in BHP Billiton have been massive performers, up 38% in six months, but we only have 100 of them. K.P. Sharma's deal with our departing Canadian member has left us with 200 shares in BT, 1000 in Debt Free Direct and of course 200 in Northern Rock. It's all worth just over £6500 with the small amount of cash left.

"I don't think we should have bought those Debt Free Direct shares," says Martin Gale, who has a voluntary agreement with creditors through a similar company. "It's making money out of other people's misfortune. My IVA has been a very painful experience, let me tell you."

"Tell me about it," says Harry Staines. "You haven't bought a round since Valentine's Day, but you're still as thirsty as ever."

"We have lost a bit on DFD, and it's already had a profit warning hasn't it?" I said to K.P. Sharma.

"Well, it was either hold onto that or Oakdene Homes," K.P. replied. "I didn't want us to be holding a house builder now the housing market looks to have peaked. About 90% of the portfolio was Cynthia's money, so most shares had to be sold. DFD is insurance against recession."

"But then you persuaded us to buy Northern Rock," said Chantelle, today sporting a bleached hairstyle that could best be described as 'post-tornado haystack'. "If the housing market goes down, that's going to be hard hit."

"Chantelle," K.P. said slowly, sounding slightly patronising. "You've got to differentiate between worries that are in the price and worries that aren't."

"If you'd have bought the Sunday Sport shares like I suggested, we'd have made a hundred quid by now," said Harry. "As it is we've lost a hundred on Northern Rock."

Wednesday Evening: Topham Tales

Eunice, still smarting from the hair-raising disaster at Catwalk Cuts has elected to wear a hat for the fund-raising evening at St Simeon's church. Hat is a loose description, however. Frankly, it looks like a road-killed pheasant glued onto a schoolgirl's beret. The Hon. Sir Giles and Lady Topham gave us both a wide berth, perhaps worried they may contract psittacosis from the thing.

Still, the food was good and I managed to get a few glasses of wine. Eunice fell in with her neighbour and confidante Daphne Hanson-Hart, enabling me to snaffle a couple of slices of victoria sponge without being spotted by the cholesterol cops. While I perused the hymnbooks and lectern I could hear Eunice droning away about how she would never again to be able to go to Catwalk Cuts after the way they treated her. I even spotted Daphne being given a tour of the damage under the highly un-pheasant head gear. Ever supportive, Daphne tutted in sympathy with Eunice's plight of having to find another, but equally exorbitant, hairdresser in which to squander my hard-earned money.

Thursday 13th September: Genghis Can't

In the evening on the BBC website, I read that Northern Rock has been granted an emergency loan by the Bank of England. Hang on a minute! I re-read the interim results from 25 July, and see the bank had been expanding its lending and taking market share. Surely it wouldn't do that if it didn't have the money? It has even upped the dividend because it doesn't need so much capital because of Basel II (whatever that is).

Decide to phone Perfect Peter Edgington, who should now be back from his holiday. His wife Geraldine picks up the phone, and twitters on endlessly about their trans-Siberian adventures, the exquisite jewellery she picked up in Tashkent, and the delights of travelling Tsar-class. "To be honest Bernard, the only fly in the ointment was in Ulan Bator where a Tartar taxi driver drove me off at knifepoint while Peter was loading my case in the boot."

"Did he rob you?" I asked in astonishment.

"Actually, he tried to ravish me," she said, languidly. "In an alleyway. By an open sewer. Fortunately, I always keep my Chanel No 5 atomiser to hand, and a spray of that in the eyes had Genghis in rapid retreat. The High Commission was wonderful about it. The commissioner's wife lent me her pashmina while I had mine cleaned. Otherwise that would have been a real crisis."

While I'm still stunned by this aristocratic adventure, she promises that Peter will read up on the news and ring me back.

Friday 14th September: Edgington To The Rescue

I'm on the computer by 8am, and Northern Rock shares are in freefall from the bell, 480p! At five past, Perfect Peter phones up with the one word advice – sell. Of course, but I need to get hold of K.P. Sharma, who holds our club account details on his laptop. Ring his house, but Mrs Sharma says he's out. Try his mobile and leave a message. Panic is now in charge. I try ringing Harry Staines, but his long-suffering spouse Avril says he's driven off to Bromley in great haste.

"Why?" I ask.

"Well, we've got our savings at the Northern Rock and that's the nearest branch. I think he's in a big queue."

Realise then that Eunice has an account at Northern Rock too, though I've no idea how much she has in it. She's watching repeats of *Emmerdale*, and I know better than to disturb her, especially if all I'm going to do is inflame her anxiety.

Ring Peter again, and explain the situation. As always, he has an answer. "Alright, Bernard. Here's what I'll do. I've got an old CFD account and I'll take a short-selling position on Northern Rock to the same amount as the share club is long, which should hedge any further downward exposure at least until you can sell. I'll bail out the share club with my profits, but if it recovers they'll have to cover my losses, okay?"

Marvellous! Oh, how I wish I were as clever as Perfect Peter Edgington. We're stuck owning something we don't want to own, but cannot for the moment sell. He doesn't own any, but by going short can sell them, effectively insuring us against any future losses.

Chapter Two

Minimum Wage

Saturday 15th September: Bank Run

Eunice was thrown into a complete lather by the Northern Rock news, which I broke to her over breakfast. She recalls having a Northern Rock account years ago, but has lost the passbook and can't find any statements. I ask her how much was in it.

"I don't know, Bernard. It could be fifteen or sixteen thousand. I know that when Mummy died I sold her furniture and most of the big family paintings and put the proceeds in there."

She tries phoning Northern Rock customer services and I try the website, but one is busy, the other down. Eunice is particularly frustrated because she is due to help Daphne Hanson-Hart set up her watercolour exhibition at the library in twenty minutes' time. Daphne's 'Estuary at Twilight' looked to me more like 'Explosion at Used Pampers Recycling Plant' but it inexplicably sold for £200, and Eunice is desperate to be a part of it.

"The government has guaranteed all deposits, so you've nothing to worry about," I tell her.

"My God, you really were born yesterday, weren't you?" she says, slipping on her 'look-I'm-in-a-trendy-art-set' Chinese embroidered jacket. "Remember 'Yes, Minister'? Never believe anything until it has been officially denied. I'm going to get my money back if I have to queue for a week."

Of course, it looks like it's yours truly who will be investing a week lying in a sleeping bag on a dog-mess and chewing gum besmirched pavement in Bromley. I am delegated to go through Eunice's papers, get the account number and hold a place in the queue at the branch until she arrives. My papers, of course, are neatly arranged in alphabetical order in a filing cabinet in Lemon Curdistan. Eunice's, so she shouts to me as she is leaving, are in with the *Cosmopolitan* magazines under the bed.

So at 10am, I am digging through carrier bags full of *Cosmopolitan*, *Elle*, *Marie Claire* and other vacuous glossy rubbish. Here there are competitions to win a new erogenous zone, a prize draw for an urn containing the contents of George Clooney's electric razor, and an article on ten ways to make a man cry your name in bed (but no mention of burning his model railway, which strikes me as the most obvious). Finally, I find a gift box tied with string. Undoing it, I expect to see bank statements, but am instead confronted with what I presume to be a marital aid. This blue rubbery object has more buttons than a Hornby points controller and some strange 'bits' on the side, with two tiny fingers arranged in a rude gesture. It actually reminds me of an emaciated Smurf. I press one button and the thing vibrates so much it jumps out of my hand. Another button and it wiggles up and down like some pornographic caterpillar. So this explains the mystery £47 Ann Summers credit card bill. More shocking still, I see my wife has a copy of *Playgirl*, which a quick flick through shows to be far more racy than I imagined.

I quickly stash this terrifying stuff back in the box, and with shaking hands resume my search for Northern Rock material. Eventually, in a tatty envelope, I find an old Northern Rock passbook, circa 1992 with a total at that date of £12,837 credited. With a renewed sense of urgency I jump into the Volvo and set off for Bromley.

Sunday 16th September: All For Nought

Stood for four and a half hours yesterday in a very British queue. All types represented, from the Muslim student with his bursary to protect, to a Bermondsey florist hoping to withdraw her life savings. Plus one befuddled old-school fellow in a blazer, who planned to move his mortgage to a safer bank. The staff, cheery despite the prospect of job cuts, were kindly handing out tea and coffee. I'm sure they are as much in shock as the rest of us. Eunice arrived at 3.40pm, with immaculate timing, just as I was making it inside the branch.

When we finally got to the front, the poor cashier looked worn out. She typed in the account number, looked up and announced: "That's £16.22. Would you like to withdraw it all?"

While Eunice quibbled and blustered, I tottered outside where I found a convenient piece of wall next to the cashpoint and started banging my head gently against it.

"It's no good needling me about it," Eunice said when we were on the way home. "I can't be expected to remember that I transferred it into the Halifax in 1998, can I?" She flicked through the statement they had printed out for her.

"But why didn't you close the account?" I wailed. "At least we wouldn't have these odds and ends knocking around. For the amount of time I spent queuing yesterday, the balance doesn't even amount to minimum wage."

"Certainly not. One doesn't pay one's husband for what should be an act of love and solidarity," Eunice said crisply.

Tuesday 18ᵗʰ September: Hedge Trimming

Thank goodness that Peter Edgington has so kindly hedged the share club's exposure to Northern Rock. By the time I'd got hold of K.P. Sharma to sell the shares on Monday, the price had plummeted to 280p. However, Peter's short-sell CFD kicked in from 460p on Friday, so we've 'only' lost, um: 718p minus 460p, which is...258p per share. With 200 shares that is £516 of club funds down the drain, but it could easily have been double. How I wish, for once, that we had listened to Harry Staines and bought shares in the publisher of the *Sunday Sport*.

Wednesday 19th September: Robbing Peter

Share club meeting starts with a little self-congratulation for the money that we have saved, courtesy of Peter, and a vote of thanks to him. Only Harry looks smug, having had nothing to do with out disastrous Northern Rock foray. K.P. Sharma is particularly relieved, seeing as it was his recommendation.

"So what price did Peter close out his short position at then, Bernard?" K.P. asks.

"I don't know. I presume you checked that with him to coordinate closing both positions," I reply.

"No, Bernard, I didn't have time. I just sold our Northern Rock shares. You were down as the coordinator. You didn't ring him?"

"Er, no. I thought you would," I say.

"Are you saying that he's still running the position?" Chantelle says. We all crowd around K.P.'s laptop while he checks the price. Northern Rock shares are now down at 255p.

"Hang on, is that good or bad for us?" I ask.

"It's good," says K.P. "But it would be very bad if the price started to climb above 280p, because then Peter's profits would no longer exceed the losses we made from 460p downwards."

"But we wanted the price to go up," I say, now thoroughly confused.

"Yes, Bernard," said K.P. testily. "When we owned them and before the hedge. But now we've sold we are, via Peter, naked short, rather than hedged."

I have a headache coming on and take a deep draught of my Damson Porter, a rather fine guest ale that does nothing to clear my head. There follows five minutes of mind-boggling argy-bargy about profits and losses until Chantelle says: "What's his number?"

"Whose?" K.P. asks.

"Peter Edgington's. Don't you think we should ring him?"

We all agree this is the top priority, but tapping my jacket I realise I don't have my address book with me. Chantelle tries the directory by the payphone, but being the Ring o'Bells, most pages have been ripped to shreds. K.P. tries BT's free online directory, but he's not in it. It's now 4.10pm and Eunice hasn't returned my call. She finally does so, with perfect timing at 4.31pm.

"Thank you so much," I say as she relays Peter's number.

"Don't be sarky, Bernard. If you'd taken your book..."

"The market's just closed, that's the bloody problem."

Eunice hangs up on me. So I draw a deep breath and call Peter. He is understandably testy, despite my apologies.

"That was not the idea, was it? I was doing you all a big favour," he says. "Let's just hope there's no bid for it tomorrow."

Thursday 20th September: Edgington Triumphs Again

9am. Peter rings and, somewhat jubilantly, announces that he has closed his short position on Northern Rock at 176p.

"Oh, right," I respond, trying to work out whether that is good for the club or for him. "Are you happy?" I ask cautiously.

"Naturally," he says. "I've covered your club positions down from 460p to 280p, and at 176p that's an extra 104p per share profit just for me. Quite honestly, this isn't my kind of investing, but it was in its own way quite exciting. I've saved the Ring o'Bells share club £360, and I've made over £200 for myself."

Saturday 22nd September: Pomegranate Promise

Blissful day all to myself on the model railway, staging a re-enactment of the notorious Bristol Temple Meads derailment of 1909. Eunice is out at yet another event to raise lolly for a new roof at St Simeon's. Apparently, the soaring price of lead keeps pushing the target ever higher. Perhaps they should just have bought shares in BHP Billiton. Still, for the amount of auctioned marrows, beetroot and courgettes jamming our fridge you'd have thought you could have re-roofed St Paul's Cathedral in gold leaf.

Eunice arrives at 4pm: "I've got some pumpkin and pomegranate chutney from the WI tombola. It's supposed to be marvellous for your prostate," she said, waving the jar towards me. "Oh for goodness sake, Bernard, stop looking horrified. You're supposed to eat it, you don't have to insert the jar."

Monday 24th September: Halo Slips

Brian tells me that Digby has been pestering him and Janet non-stop for a fortnight to get him an X-Box so he can play some new video game called Halo 3. What either of these things are I cannot tell you, but no child is 'cool' without them, so my schoolteacher son tells me. I lost touch with toys when Meccano finally died out, and am shocked to be told it will cost £299 for console and game.

"That's a heck of a Christmas present," I say.

"Oh no. It can't wait for Christmas, I'm afraid," Brian responds. "It came out today, and that's when he wants it. You know what he's like if he doesn't get his way. Frankly it's worth it for a bit of peace and quiet. Still, it'll have to go on plastic."

Well, if Brian runs his classroom like he runs his home, no wonder our schools are in such a state. Once again it seems that Digby, the pint-size demon, has his parents on a string. In the meantime I look up Halo 3 on the Internet, and I'm amazed. The future of the latest X-box player hangs on this game, which Microsoft has spent more promoting than if it was a Hollywood blockbuster. Actually, it isn't so daft when you realise it has more in common with a film than a game. It just happens to be a film where you control the characters. You can even play an online version. No wonder Microsoft's shares have risen as the reviews emerged.

11.30pm. Eunice comes down to Lemon Curdistan to find me. "Bernard, you've missed that Channel 5 programme you wanted to watch about life in Northamptonshire's public health department."

Damn. I'd been looking forward to *Dysentery in Daventry*.

"So what are you doing? You're cocoa's been waiting for two hours. It's stone cold."

"I'm looking for hunters," I tell her. "I've got two down so far, but I've taken a hit from a plasma gun and I've got to get the sergeant back to a field hospital."

"For goodness sake. It's bad enough that you play trains all day long in the loft, now when I think you're trying to secure our retirement it turns out you are playing cowboys and Indians. If you're regression to childhood continues at this rate I'm getting you a shape sorter for Christmas."

Wednesday 26th September: Traumatic For Some

Hell's Bell's share club meeting. K.P. Sharma brandishes a copy of the *FT* and shows us a full page story on Chinese pork prices. "Isn't that amazing?" he says.

"Yeah," says Harry Staines. "The Golden Wheel's now charging £7.85 for ribs in sweet and sour sauce, and when that miserable cow's there you only get three in a box. My missus has always preferred the chicken anyway."

"No, what I mean is that the trend of meat consumption, animal supply and farmyard diseases in China is now recognised as a real force in global commodity prices. Isn't that an amazing development?" K.P. said.

I agree with him, but can't decide how we in suburban North Kent can play this particular trend.

"How about buying a commodity fund?" Martin Gale asks.

"We need to take a rigorous approach though," says Chantelle, as she cleans the counter of the Ring o'Bells food bar. "Pig prices are going up not just because the Chinese can now afford to eat more meat, but due to the cost of feed. And that's going up because the American's are turning corn into ethanol."

Impressed by this analysis, we wait for more. Our barmaid-cum-investor today has orange and purple hair, black lipstick and three rivets just above each collarbone. She looks like an escapee from an Andrew Lloyd-Webber musical.

"All I'm saying is pricey pork doesn't mean easy money from investing in pigs," she adds.

"What about pig-breeding?" we hear a Yorkshire voice say. Standing at the bar is a small bloke in overalls, with a thin face and bad teeth. "That Genus company makes money from pigs, like, as well as cows. I've done well with them shares."

Harry waves him over to join us, and he introduces himself as Russell Traugh. Only then do I see the logo on his overalls: 'TraughMatic Ltd: Your local abrasive experience.'

Russell, it seems, is a self-made man whose experience of business, which he is delighted to share with us unprompted, comes down to one thing. "It's cash in your pocket, money in the bank and nowt more. Get cashflow right and you're more n'halfway."

He stays for a while, asks about what's in the club portfolio, but then wanders off after finishing the pint that Harry bought him.

"Should we let him join if he's interested?" asks K.P.

"I'd wait to see if he buys a round," says Harry. "One tightwad like Martin is enough for any share club."

Chapter Three

Sooty And Sweep

Thursday 4th October: Glove Puppets Off

After Halo 3, what future for Sooty? I read that privately-owned Hit Entertainment and Guinness Flight, joint owners of Sooty and Sweep, are selling up having given up hope of selling foreign rights to the glove puppets' TV show. Thousands of bored children would not be surprised to hear that Guinness Flight had already slashed the equity value of the brand to £324,000 from £2 million. Why it's still worth that baffles me. Still, it's the end of an era. That kind of direct entertainment which doesn't actually need a screen now seems like something out of the dark ages. Perhaps I should look for something in my portfolio that reflects that future.

Wednesday 10th October: Taxing Admiration

Hell's Bell's share club is off to a slow start. Harry is checking odds in the *Racing Post*, making careful notes in the margin.

"You'll never get rich that way," K.P. Sharma says.

"I'll never get rich the other way either," Harry retorts through a mouthful of cheese and pickle roll. "I've just got two words to say about the share club's recommendations: 'Northern' and 'Rock'."

Just then, our friend Russell walks in wearing cheap glossy tracksuit trousers that whistle while he walks. Ever the self-publicist, he's wearing a TraughMatic Ltd T-shirt.

"You all broke yet?" he chuckles.

"Soon will be if you don't buy a round," Harry mutters.

Russell gets himself a pint and sits down at the table to look at K.P.'s laptop. "What y'got 'ere then?"

"Losses," says Martin Gale. "Apart from BHP Billiton, which is doing very nicely."

"I'm not surprised. Harry here can't even add up."

"I certainly can," Harry said. "In fact every year the Inland Revenue writes to me to tell me how good my tax return is."

"Really?" says Chantelle, clearly shocked.

"Can't believe it," says K.P. Sharma.

Harry smirked. "Every February they say: 'Dear Mr Staines, we have to tell you that once again your tax return is outstanding'."

After the laughter has subsided, even Russell gives in and buys a round. However, when it arrives it turns out to be halves and not pints.

Thursday 11th October: A Sharp Fall

My mother phones up at 6am and says she's poorly.

I can hardly hear her voice. Alarmingly, it turns out she had a fall yesterday and didn't tell me. "What happened, Mum?"

"Well, I was in Boots and I got Maurice stuck in foot care. It's a bit tight there, and I normally reverse into toiletries. This time there wasn't room because of this fat woman on a chair waiting for a prescription. So the lady from pharmacy said I should do a U-turn in feminine hygiene. But I got my arm caught on the Durex display and when I turned it pulled me out the seat, and I fell on me hip. My first thought was: that's me prolapse gone again. Anyway, it wasn't. They sorted me out and got me home in an ambulance. But this morning I had a funny turn."

I was more than a bit concerned about this, and interrupted the medical minutiae to tell her I would go around to Isleworth and bring her to stay with us for a couple of days. After interminable delays on the M25 I arrived to find her looking very pale, sitting up in bed with reams of handwritten notes around her.

"You're wearing Geoffrey's old glasses again, aren't you?" I said gently. "Now what's all this stuff then?"

"I'm re-doing me will. I though I better had," she said tearfully. "I'm not long for this world."

A fist tightened in my heart. I looked at the sheaf of paper, threaded with indecipherable spidery scrawl. "May I look?"

She nodded. The first thing I saw was 'Donkey Sanctuary.' How much she was leaving it I couldn't decipher.

"Mum. Don't you think we should get Mr Ridley to do it for you? This is very untidy and hard to understand."

I picked up another page and read just one clear sentence. 'I leave my zebra hide ottoman and £500 to Maurice.'

"You can't leave a pouf to your mobility vehicle! Or cash, for that matter. It's not even a cat! It's entirely inanimate!"

"He could do with a new seat cover. Zebra would look nice."

This is clearly more serious than I thought. Sound mind? Not a bit of it. I wonder where the original will is, and ask her. She points to the bedside cabinet, and there it is, in an envelope from Mr Ridley of Ridley, Gryp and Poultice. I open it with trembling hands and see a neat 15-page document, but also notice it has been snipped at. There are all sorts of neat little holes in it.

"What on earth is this?" I ask, poking my finger through one of many holes.

"I said I'd cut you out, didn't I? Well I did."

Friday 12th October: Wilful Behaviour

Can't believe my mother cut me out of her will...with scissors! I showed this doily of a document to Eunice yesterday, who thought it the funniest thing she'd ever seen. Still, now she's laughing on the other side of her face as Dot is here to recuperate from her fall. She's only been here 24 hours and is driving us to distraction. First it was getting up at 3.30am to peel parsnips for dinner. Then it was looking under the bed at 4.15am for Uncle Harold's terrapin (which was actually incinerated by an incendiary bomb in 1940, along with Harold's priceless collection of Boer War cummerbunds, and yes, we reminded her, poor Harold himself). Finally, after a few hours kip I awoke at 7am to persistent prodding to see Dot standing over me wearing a gas mask and not a lot else. I screamed in terror (as anyone would). Even when I had regained my composure, her urgent mumbling remained incomprehensible. I pulled the mask off her head, leaving her hair in frightening vertical wisps.

"Why hasn't the siren gone off? A V2 just landed!"

"I think that'll just be the bin men, Dot," Eunice said, blearily.

"But Bernard, there was a huge bang!"

"Yes," I explained. "Daphne Hanson-Hart's recycling bin. The bin men don't like Daphne because of her year-long refusal to accept a bin. Now after emptying it, they like to throw it into her drive from the back of the lorry to make a point. That's all."

Tuesday 16th October: Breathing Again

Dot, now feeling better, has been ferried home and I can breathe again. However, it's clear that she will soon have to go into a home. Whether I'm in her will or not, the cost of a few year's specialised care will make Northern Rock's overdraft at the Bank of England look like chicken feed. My own portfolio is worth a miserable £93,000. With current annuity rates the income wouldn't be enough to cover council tax and utilities. But Dot's invested assets, even assuming the £150,000 she passed to Jem is now lost to civilisation, are still about half a million. Add the house and she'll be over £1 million. That's enough to buy a second home in the Dordogne, two more holidays every year, and a new car, a Jaguar even. Maybe a bit of cosmetic surgery for Eunice. Liposuction, perhaps, if that is where they glue them together. The only trouble would be keeping her face immobile long enough for the Araldite to set.

I must redouble my efforts over the will. I'll phone her solicitor tomorrow. If my soppy daughter Jem can get money out of the daft old bat, so can I. It's just a question of working out how.

Wednesday 17ᵗʰ October: Careless Homes

I suggested to the share club that we should buy shares in the care home sector. I talk enthusiastically about the demographics, the consolidation the sector is likely to have and the attractive cash generation.

"I don't agree," says Mike Delaney. "My dad went into a so-called care home which was just run for the money. They didn't have enough staff to feed all the residents, and his dinner often got taken away before he'd had a chance to have any."

There's a bit of shock at Mike's uncharacteristic intervention, until Harry says: "Looks like we just started an ethical investment club, doesn't it?"

Monday 22nd October: Toby Back Again

A quiet evening with the model railway, a signal box and some Humbrol was in prospect. Eunice was on a witch's night out with numerous basket-weaving, braid-making and macramé-torturing cronies, presumably just a dry run for Halloween. It wasn't to be. Jem turned up unexpectedly with a surprise guest: Toby.

The fop-haired former boyfriend and City trader, whose sexual ambiguity is one of life's great mysteries, is now interested in girls again. Well hooray. He's wooed Jem with, of all things, a black labrador puppy, and it seems to have worked.

So while I ply them with toasted cheese and Valpolicella, and tickle the charming and so-far unnamed puppy, the story unfolds. No mention is made of course of the £150,000 advance on her grandmother's will she so effortlessly secured, or how much of it found its way into paying off Toby's huge debts, or what has happened to the unsaleable Spanish property Toby bought with his mascara-wearing ex-boyfriend Carlos. All Jem has to tell is that their on-again, off-again, relationship is now on. To prove it they canoodle embarrassingly on the sofa, and stare into each other's eyes. Quite embarrassed by this, I find enthusiasm for washing the grill pan. The only plus I can see is that Jonathan, Jem's randy and lugubrious boss, and a married man, has been seen off. This may well be at some cost to Jem's legal career. Yes, now she's returned to the dandy, there's little chance of a beano.

Tuesday 23rd October: Lawyer, Lawyer Pants On Fire

Eunice is out, and I'm just tucking into a slice of Swiss roll, when the phone rings and an adenoidal woman says: "Hold for Mr

Ridley." The solicitor I rang for an urgent chat about my mother's will almost a week ago has just deigned to return my call, or has deigned to let me listen to 'hold' music, an irritating glockenspiel rendition of Elton John singing *Goodbye Yellow Brick Road*. Which, insofar as it concerns a Krugerrand carriageway to inheritance, seems to describe my situation perfectly. After five minutes of this a bored and laconic voice comes on the line: "Ridley."

"Ah, Herbert. It's about my mother's will. Did you know she's taken a pair of scissors to it?"

"I'm sorry I don't know what you're talking about." I start to give him the details, until he interrupts. "Mr Jones. I'm not at liberty to discuss your mother's legal affairs with you, or anyone else. I have a copy of her most recent will, and it's perfectly in order."

"But has she changed it recently…"

"As I say, I'm not at liberty to discuss it. Should I be notified of any unfortunate circumstances vis-a-vis her ongoing survival, I would as executor be in touch with family and relevant friends."

"But you've been our family solicitor for 40 years."

"Well, yes. But in this matter I cannot advise you, and you would need another firm. I've heard that Mrs Harris at Khan and Singh is rather good. Good day!"

Wednesday 24th October: Split Over Bank Prospects

Share club at the Ring o'Bells is pre-occupied with BHP results, which missed expectations after cost over-runs and some production problems. It's our best performing stock, but clearly we need others. BT is steady but unexciting, while Debt Free Direct is in a steady downtrend, despite expectations of economic gloom.

"I think it's time to look at banks again," said K.P. Sharma. "There are such bargains out there, really unprecedented."

"Might I remind you about Northern Rock?" Harry said. "A bargain, you said. Couldn't fail, you said. We lost hundreds on it."

"Yes, but look at Bradford & Bingley or Barclays. They don't have the same problem at all. B&B fell below 250p on Monday! That's a potential yield of nearly 8%."

"What if it doesn't make its numbers?" said Chantelle. "I think we should wait until the trading updates at the end of November."

K.P. doesn't, and neither does Martin Gale, who seems drawn to risk like a moth to a flame. Mike Delaney and I cast our votes with Harry and Chantelle, which defeats the move to buy banks by four-to-two. Divided, we once again bought nothing.

Thursday 25th October: Return Of The Elevenses

The stock market continues to behave oddly, caning builders and banks, and rewarding commodity plays. Fretting over this, I seek elevenses at the unusually early hour of 9.30am. Opening up Prescott, the suede pig in whose stuffing I had concealed a packet of chocolate digestives, I find just an apple, left there by you-know-who. Oh God. Now I'm for it. Eunice confronts me at lunch.

"Bernard, I'm really tired of you behaving like a naughty schoolboy. Hiding things from me, as if I won't find out." She pauses and then gives me that dangerous hippopotamus look as she bites into a high food-miles Peruvian nectarine.

"You know, Bernard. It's really time you started to grow up. To behave like a man. Take me out to dinner, woo me under starlight, hold me close in your arms. Do you know, Marjorie Fielding at baskets said that Lionel made passionate love to her on the kitchen table during *Antiques Roadshow*?"

I remind Eunice that our self-assembled MFI kitchen table trembles under the buttering of a toasted teacake. It's hardly likely to survive the amorous passions of a size-16 woman, antique or otherwise. As a compromise I suggest taking her out to dinner at the new Italian restaurant that has opened in town.

So, at 8pm we arrive at Capo Tomaso's, which turns out to be a Mafia-themed pizza joint with pounding music, where the waiters have dark glasses and trilbies and the waitresses are mini-skirted molls (or perhaps trolls). Assailed by the din of Motörhead, I eventually ask for a little Omerta. Our gangly waitress flips through their CD collection. "We don' ave. Marilyn Manson, okay?"

Hastily paying the bill, we're home by 9.30pm. As I pull into the drive, and turn off the engine Eunice suddenly hits the recline lever on my seat. As I pitch backwards, there is a squeal of faux leather, some grumbling about gear sticks and the final arrival on my midriff of a vast amount of extra wifely weight. Wriggling for breath, all I can manage to say is: "But *Antiques Roadshow* isn't on until Sunday!"

Chapter Four

Pizza The Action

Thursday 1st November: Cheesed Off

Up early, having slept well, despite Eunice's arrival at 2am from a Halloween evening out (bound to include a trip on the broomstick). Fortunately, my feigned unconsciousness was enough to avert any hippopotamus manoeuvres. She's made no attempts since that appalling episode in the Volvo last week.

My good mood lasts until I log onto my PC and notice Domino's Pizza shares have fallen 40p to 200p after a trading update. With a 14% jump in like-for-like sales, the only possible bad news is the increased cost of cheese. How ridiculous! This market is scared of its own shadow. Domino's was about my only share that was really performing this year. Hornby's down by 25% since August and QinetiQ has frankly been a disaster.

Cheesed off I may be, but Eunice is full of beans. While I struggle at breakfast with my Waitrose organic Namibian grapefruit, she regales me with tales of how her basket-weaving cronies last night painted the town puce.

"How many of you were arrested?" I ask.

"None, Bernard. But we did find this dishy young constable who Daphne wanted to take home. She almost got him into a taxi."

"Poor chap, had he known it would involve a whole night listening to the horrors of council wheelie bin policy, he'd have handcuffed himself to a lamppost to avoid it."

At this moment, I open a letter from the garage and almost choke. The bill for fixing the Volvo is £386 plus VAT!

"See what your carnal capers cost?" I say, waving the letter.

"I thought it was just the broken seat recline thingy. What's this about 'burned out window motors'?" she asked.

"It's hardly surprising is it? I mean we're parked in our own drive at midnight with the windows, front and rear, going up and down for five minutes and I'm too squashed to do a thing about it."

"Well, I got my knee stuck on the window buttons when I was straddling you. There's really no room in that car."

"And the horn jammed on where your giant derrière was wedged against it. I mean, thank God you'd not managed to get our clothes undone by the time the Pendlewoods arrived to see what was going on. I'm sure we'll never live it down."

"It's not too big, is it?" Eunice said, standing before the mirror.

"What?"

"My derrière. You said it was enormous."

"Giant, actually. Well, only that it kept setting the horn off."

"Bernard, is giant bigger than enormous, or smaller?"

"For God's sake, woman, it's this bloody bill which is enormous. You're 59-years old and I really don't care if you've got a bum the size of Hanger Lane Gyratory System so long as I don't have to find hundreds of pounds to get the car fixed."

And then, quite inexplicably, she burst into tears and fled the room. I will never understand women, not if I live to be a thousand.

Saturday 3rd November: Gleaming Spires

Finally chipped the last of the egg off the porch from Halloween. Bloody kids. Speaking of which, Brian and Janet arrived with our 'delightful' nine-year-old grandson, Digby. His sullen countenance, caused this time by the school's confiscation of his mobile phone (for filming a gang attack on another pupil), does nothing to encourage me in discussing with Brian what should be done to invest for Digby's university education. We long ago started a saving plan for him which will mature when he's 18, by which time he'll undoubtedly use it to buy Semtex, AK47s and credit card cloning equipment. Being an international master criminal will be much more his style than taking PPE at Oxford, and a damn sight cheaper. Indeed, after a miserable performance by the Scunthorpe & Skegness Building Society Child Education Bond, the only education it could buy would be a two-day course at the local community college in doner kebab handling and hygiene. Seeing as I've been putting in £1 a week for five years, I think we've been mis-sold, again.

In the afternoon, I phoned Perfect Peter Edgington to ask his advice, which was quite simple: "Start him a stakeholder pension wrapped around a cheap tracker fund, Bernard. He won't be able to touch it until he's old and sensible, you get tax relief on the contributions and it'll have six decades to turn your £1 a week into a really sizeable sum." Well, what a good idea!

Sunday 4th November: Buns Of Steel

Eunice brandishes a DVD at me: "Look, I've borrowed *Buns of Steel* from Irmgard."

"Oh God, not more organic home baking," I wailed. "I've told you before those multi-grain loaves kill my teeth."

"Don't be silly, Bernard. It's an exercise course. I won't have you complaining about my bottom again."

Tuesday 6ᵗʰ November: A Trip Down Clio Lane

A trading update from Bovis, the one house builder in my portfolio, shows life is getting tougher. The average selling price of its homes is now likely to be 3% lower than a year ago. Each time when the share price falls I think it is too late to sell, and each time it falls more. Bovis stood at 1200p at its peak in April, and now it is barely half that. I can't believe I bought more in the summer at 925p, nor how much less they are now worth. A little glummer than usual at breakfast, I was startled to see Eunice reading the financial pages of the *Daily Mail*.

"What is all this sub-prime lending, Bernard? Is it affecting our nest egg? Will there be a recession? And what's stagflation?"

I do my best to explain, and reassure her that everything's fine. I do not mention that the portfolio is only worth more this year because of the extra cash I've put in it. Without that it would be down 8%. I'm pleased to see she's reassured.

"Bernard, you do such a good job for us," she strokes my hand, before turning back to the paper. "I presume it's okay about me getting a new Clio, then?" she slips out innocently, while turning the page to Femail.

"What!" I splutter, spraying coffee and crumbs over the *Telegraph*. "The current one's only three years old."

"But, Bernard, Irmgard's just got a new Audi. And the paint's beginning to come off where I knocked it in Waitrose."

"Which knock? There were three as I recall."

"Well, exactly. I can't have everyone at baskets thinking we're hard up. Anyway, so I've chosen a nice kingfisher blue one."

"Are you telling me that this is a fait accompli?"

"If you mean 'have I decided?', the answer is yes."

"And what will you use for money, pray?"

"Bernard, I don't need your money. I've got a L-O-A-N.

"And how are you going to meet the R-E-P-A-Y-M-E-N-T-S? Have you suddenly started earning an I-N-C-O-M-E?"

"It's actually quite easy. I put the deposit down on plastic and got a £2000 trade-in on the old one. Loan repayments are over five years, some of which I can pay from my pension."

The next forty minutes descends into a row in which my key subjects of APR ("What's that, Bernard?") and depreciation ("pardon?") are gradually replaced by hers: old skinflint ("That's what you've always been, Bernard") and lack of love ("If you loved me more, I wouldn't have to cheer myself by spending"). The end result, though, is that I will have to foot the bill for a top-of-the-range 1.5 litre diesel limited edition hatchback with satnav and a bloody iMusic system of all things.

Wednesday 7ᵗʰ November: Dented Sweepstake

I take my tale of woe to the Share Club but get nothing but laughter from Harry Staines and Martin Gale, even when I mention the rip-off trade-in price. K.P. Sharma tells me I'm lucky, his wife went out and bought a four-wheel drive BMW before she'd even taken her test. He tells me she's on re-take number six now and the thing has already lost £12,000 in value.

"Listening to this makes me think I should have bought shares in Accident Exchange," Chantelle says. "Clearly someone's making money out of people like Eunice."

"Tell you what," says Harry. "Let's have a sweepstake: how long before Eunice dents the new one. I reckon before Christmas."

This is too painful, and I tell him so, but everyone else is up for it. Russell Traugh, who senses discomfort like a vulture finds dead meat, looks up from his pint of Worthington's. His nylon trousers making a sound like frying bacon as he sidles over.

"My missus never makes money out of me," he says.

"I don't imagine too many people do," Martin responds.

"I bought her a second-hand moped in 1983 and taught her how to maintain it herself," he says with grim satisfaction.

"And I suppose it's still running as good as ever?" I say.

"Oh no. It was totally bloody ruined when the old bat pulled out in front of a concrete mixer in 1985. Well, not totally, I sold the gearbox and tyres to me brother for £40, like."

"But what about your poor wife?" K.P. Sharma asks.

"Nah, he wouldn't take her. Not without legs, like. But I got her disability living allowance, carer's allowance and attendance allowance. We're quids in."

"I don't think I'd like to be married to you," Chantelle says.

"What do you mean? I'm kind!" Russell says indignantly. "I even invested in a specially adapted vehicle to meet her needs."

"That's not what you told me," says Harry. "You said you built a plywood ramp for your old Transit, and bung her in the back in her wheelchair to rattle around with the grinders and sanding discs on her fortnightly outing to Asda."

I wish Eunice could hear this. She doesn't know she's born.

Thursday 15th November: Dental Disaster

I wish I'd never made the joke about 'buns of steel'. Eunice has started visiting health food shops again. Last year it was lentils and dried fruit, this time it's organic bread. The stuff is as dense as a gold brick and, with the soaring price of wheat, costs about the same. The top is scattered with what looks like Trill. Next she'll be shoving a piece of cuttlefish in my cage! She claims the fibre is good for me, but guess what? Bit into a slice of toast and marmalade this morning and crunched something that felt like gravel. Felt a sickening pain in the dodgy molar. Bloody thing's has been grumbling for months, but this time a huge lump of filling came out. Hardly surprising, got so much of this metal amalgam in my head that I should be able to pick up Radio 4. If only I'd gone for gold. When I had most of my fillings done in the 'fifties, gold was just $30 an ounce. I'd have made 20 times my money by now.

Naturally, can't get an emergency appointment at my own dentist. So instead of reading up on a busy morning of results, I spend all morning sitting in A&E waiting for the hospital wallahs to give me a temporary filling. Cost me a fiver just to leave the Volvo in the hospital car park. That really is a stealth tax.

Monday 19th November: Kitty Catch

When I was at the MoD, each of us in the department used to chip in 50p a week each into a jar for biscuits to go with the tea and coffee. We called it a kitty, and it rarely let it build up to more than a tenner, especially after we caught Sandy Douglas in Procurement helping himself both to the jar and our stockpile of garibaldis. However, Vodafone's Arun Sarin has a different idea of what constitutes loose change. He referred to a $13 billion stake in China Mobile as a 'kitty' which can be used to buy into a restructured Chinese telecoms market, presumably in much the same way we used to buy chocolate digestives. I'm not sure how much dosh would actually be required to make Mr Sarin use the phrase 'a colossal wad'.

Tuesday 20th November: Slipped Disc

Doing my monthly back-up of the PC's hard drive, when I realised that I had mislaid my disc. Searched fruitlessly under piles of old *FT*s and *Chronic Investor* magazines. I did find an old pair of reading glasses and a rather stale jaffa cake, but no luck with the disc. Still, I'm pretty certain that I didn't post if off to the Audit Commission like some silly bugger at HM Revenue & Customs did. At least what I've lost is still within the building, contains no bank account details nor anything that could be used to further impoverish me. The nearest to embarrassment I'd face would be for the world to see the blasted moonscape of ruination that my investment portfolio has become.

Wednesday 21st November: Ukrainian Foresight

Investment club at the Ring o'Bells seems to be increasingly blighted by Russell Traugh who, when not bragging about spending his wife's disability benefits, is boasting about how much money he made in shares. So far today we've heard about the £12,562.75 he made in cattle breeder Genus, which he bought at the depths of the foot and mouth outbreak in 2001, the £16,321.16 he made from ASOS, the online clothing retailer that allows chavs to pretend they're celebrities, and the £914.29 he made from a £65 investment in plant hire firm Ashtead when it was almost bankrupt.

As Russell rustles to the bar in his shell suit, Harry turns to the rest of us in exasperation. "If he's so rich, why is he driving a 12-year-old Ford Transit?"

"And why the baler twine shoe laces?" Martin asks.

"And why can't he afford a bath?" says Chantelle, who isn't the first to notice Russell's earthy 'aroma'.

"We'll ask for a share tip. That'll test him," says K.P. Sharma. Far from being fazed by this, Russell has one right to hand.

"Alright," he says. "Here's one that is a play on rising food prices, low-cost East European land, and biofuels. It lists on AIM tomorrow, so if you want to buy into it you can. It's called Landkom, and it's going to be big."

We wait for more, and then he tells us where it's based. Ukraine. Harry and Martin burst out laughing, but Russell waits until they've calmed down.

"You'll be laughing on the other side of y'face," says Russell. "This firms going to rent 300,000 hectares of land, that's half the size of Lincolnshire and at a fraction of the cost, and will use commercial Australian-style techniques to vastly increase yields. It's an idea whose time has come, mark my words."

Chapter Five

Nasdaq The Dog

Friday 23rd November: QinetiQ Rip-Off

Absolutely incandescent. Seems that senior officials at the MoD made a 20,000% profit on their stake in QinetiQ during the sell-off. What irony that those upstairs from my old department, who were by all accounts incapable of getting anything organised on time or on budget, should turn out to be investment wizards when it comes to feathering their own nests. Seeing as the QinetiQ shares I bought are down 20%, I've helped subsidise this fiasco too. It's clear they've sold me and many thousands of other innocent investors a pup. Bugger breakfast, I'm going for a walk.

"Bernard, stop banging around and slamming doors," Eunice says. "What on earth is the matter? You've not been careless eating the wholemeal toast again, have you? Fillings *are* expensive you know, so chew more carefully."

My reply is unprintable. In fact I do have a good mind to go up to the Healthy Grains and Pulses Co-operative, and give Mrs Trilobite, or whatever the owner's name is, a piece of my mind.

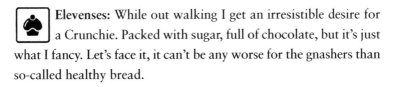 **Elevenses:** While out walking I get an irresistible desire for a Crunchie. Packed with sugar, full of chocolate, but it's just what I fancy. Let's face it, it can't be any worse for the gnashers than so-called healthy bread.

Saturday 24th November: Nasdaq The Dog

Toothache. Finally did get that fragment of Crunchie out, but the temporary filling came with it. Daren't tell Eunice what it was I was eating. She is in any case distracted by the arrival of Jemima and Toby for lunch, with their excitable black labrador puppy.

"Have you decided what to call him yet?" I ask.

"Nasdaq," says Jem. "It was Toby's idea. Because he's all over the place all the time."

It's hard to disagree with that. Like his namesake U.S. stock market index, Nasdaq is up and down like a yo-yo, with a tail that never stops wagging and a tongue longer than Eunice's credit card bill. Meanwhile Jem and Toby are still in soppy love mode, giggling, tickling and whispering like a couple of 14-year- olds. Toby is wearing a suit and tie (the latter decorated with hearts) but has, thank God, dispensed with the eyeliner and diamante earring since rediscovering heterosexuality.

After they've gone Eunice opens a second bottle of chardonnay and tells me that she's happy they're back together.

"Well, we'll see," I respond. "He's still more AC/DC than the National Grid. I really don't care, so long as he learns to look after money sensibly. There's £150,000 of Dot's money disappeared into that relationship somewhere, presumably never to re-emerge."

"That really is all you think about, isn't it? Money, money, money." Eunice drains her glass and pours another one.

"Look. You can depend on money. You can't depend on Toby. Do you hear what she calls him? Fluffy, for God's sake. He's deputy head of CDO trading, with billions of the bank's money at stake in one of the most critical times in the credit markets, and he's called Fluffy, and can't remember to pay his own mortgage."

"Well, you used to call me sweetie-pie."

"Nonsense," I say, turning to the City pages of the *Telegraph*. Eunice is already halfway down the new glass of wine.

"You did too! Sweetie-pie or Tussletops," she giggles.

"Glugzilla might have been more apposite," I say, nodding at the wine bottle.

I had thought just eating organic bread rolls painful enough. But by God, the impact is agony when thrown by an angry spouse.

Monday 26th November: Roll And Filling

Dental appointment for my broken molar finally arrived. Cow of a receptionist reminded me in imperious tones that I'd not been for 2½ years despite reminders. It wasn't neglect that broke my tooth, stupid woman. It was healthy eating. If I'd been allowed to stick to good old white Rank Hovis McDougall my gnashers wouldn't be in this state.

Seems that old Lomax has retired. They said I'd be seeing some Dr Unpronounceable. Foreigner, obviously. Waiting room's been refurbished. Nice sofas, today's papers and a telly burbling away in the corner. Must have cost a bob or two.

Anyway, get called in, bibbed up. Dr Mroczka (pronounced Muroshka) is dark haired and attractive, with lovely expressive eyes and charmingly halting English. I have to say I'm impressed. No pliers and knockout gas anymore, but videos on oral hygiene, a full explanation of what's wrong and how to fix it. Old Lomax only used to talk about cricket and socialism. The latter when I had my mouth open and couldn't reply.

Then I get the bill. No NHS work since Lomax went. This is going to be private. Four appointments, £630, she says. If my jaw hadn't already been wedged open, it would have fallen off. As I gargle my protest, I recall that there are a few listed dental shares. If there's this much money in it, I should take a look.

Tuesday 18th December: Cash Extraction

Finished my final dental appointment today, numb of mouth and empty of wallet. Two extractions and three fillings. That's most of a year's dividends on the portfolio, all gone in one chomp of granary toast. It would have been one extraction, except the charmingly attractive but overly-incentivised Dr Mroczka spotted another area of decay. While my mouth was prised open and the good dentist's sharp instrument poised to strike, I was asked to gargle my assent to *another* £175 on top of the £630 already siphoned out of my account. Unfortunately, my objections were delivered with all the eloquence of Bill and Ben the flowerpot men, though with a great deal more saliva.

"Your mouth's a big trouble, yes?" Dr Mroczka said, wiping her face. "You must look after. Or all fall out."

"May I have the extracted teeth?" I asked.

"Why do you want?"

"I'm going to put them under my pillow for the blasted tooth fairy. I used to get a shiny sixpence when I was a child, I'm just hoping that she will now oblige me with £805 now I really need it."

Wednesday 19th December: Smoking IS Good For You

Last meeting before Christmas at the Ring o'Bells, and the mood is glum. With a tender mouth, I sensibly turn down the offer of Martin Gale's pork scratchings, though I do weaken at the prospect of a slice of Chantelle's chicken and ham pie. This turns out to be a serious error, because the pastry is so hard it could have been constructed by Harland & Wolff.

"Who made any money this year?" Harry asks.

"I'm down 2%," says K.P. Sharma. "Bradford & Bingley was my biggest mistake. It could have been worse."

"Certainly would have been if we hadn't managed to get the club out of Northern Rock," Harry says.

I admit to my 11% fall, which has been made worse by a continuing and unjustified slide in Domino's Pizza.

Martin, who held iSoft shares all the way down from 390p to 58p confesses to losing about a third of his portfolio. However, he stresses that counting his 'alternative investments', which includes his Bulgarian wine rebottling venture and the looting of a BMW motorcycle from a shipwreck, he's merely lost 28%.

"I'm up 10%," grins Chantelle. "I bought Xstrata."

"What about you, Mike?" asks Martin.

Mike Delaney, holding an unlit cigar in his mouth, smiles and points a finger upwards. "45%," he whispers.

"What! You kept that quiet," Martin replies.

"I had Gallaher, which was taken over by Japan Tobacco in the April, plus BAT and National Grid. I never did a trade all year."

"Looks like fags are good for you," Martin sighed.

Monday 24th December: Christmas Shopping

All I seem to read about is the house price crash, the bank lending crisis and the personal debt catastrophe. Nobody, however, seems to have told the Great British consumer. Bluewater shopping centre is more crowded than an *Eastenders* plot. Even W.H. Smith has a queue, for goodness sake. If Kate Swann can hold off the supermarket challenge there, then perhaps someone can do it for Woolworth's too.

Eunice has refused to give me a Christmas list this year, asking me to use my 'initiative'. However, initiative is carefully fenced in. She doesn't want books, claiming they are unromantic, I daren't buy her lingerie after the allergic reaction to the Moroccan pop socks five years ago which made her feet swell up to the size of moon boots. She has outlawed cardigans and scarves because of the warehouse-full of unused ones in the spare room. I'm damned if I'll go anywhere near Ann Summers, and I can't imagine there is anything to do with basket-weaving she hasn't already got. That leaves jewellery or perfume. I take a deep breath and lurch into the House of Fraser. At the perfume counter is a six-foot toothpick dipped in face powder which I must presume to be a female member of staff.

"I'd like to get my wife some perfume," I say with as much insouciance as I can muster.

"Atomiser?"

"After my shopping experience today I'd certainly be tempted," I respond. "If House of Fraser has the plutonium,"

"No, atomiser or spray? Perfume or eau de toilette?"

"Haven't the foggiest. Nothing too smelly, though."

"What about this?" the stick insect says, spraying a blast of some noxious substance onto a sample card. This brings on a terrible coughing fit, during which a chair is procured for me until my lungs recover and my eyes stop streaming.

"Good grief what was that?" I wheeze, tears streaming down my face. "Ypres Saint Laurent?"

"No, it's Curious, by Britney Spears. It's a top-seller. You're probably just allergic."

Allergic? To Christmas shopping, certainly.

Chapter Six

Crème De La Crème

Tuesday 25th December: Christmas Mourning

Had a lovely dream that I outperformed the FTSE 100 by 70%, by investing in funeral firms. However, while drowning in cash, kept feeling a great and immovable weight as if my own coffin lid was closing on top of me. Awoke to find it was Eunice, all varicose veins and seasonal suet, girding up for a festive hippopotamus manoeuvre. I now know how Alliance & Leicester feels: a tad short on liquidity, but resigned to the credit crunch.

Staggered up an hour later for the full family fiasco. The fridge, garage and freezer in the shed were each packed to overflowing with food after four Waitrose trips in the last week. Still, you can never have enough, as I was to discover. I walked into the kitchen to find my good wife with her forearm inserted into a bald, trussed and understandably distraught ostrich.

"Bernard, I don't think we've got enough whipping cream. Would you nip out to the Spar and get some?"

"But I'm sure we have cream." I gingerly opened the fridge, and dismantled a vertical wall of produce to uncover two pints of double cream, a half pint of half-fat pouring cream, a tub of extra-thick Cornish, a pot of crème fraiche, two cartons of long-life single cream and a carton of organic plain yoghurt. "Look at all this..."

"Bernard, look, I'm busy enough as you can see...."

At this point Digby burst into the kitchen shooting us with his MegaBattleStarDeathWand, which each time the trigger was pressed squawked: "You're dead meat, sucker." Oddly, he failed to shoot the turkey, which would at least have rendered its electronic proclamations accurate.

"We'll manage," I continued. "Please, give poor supermarkets this one special day to recover. I mean, what you do to them isn't shopping, it's corporate stalking."

At the Spar shop, one spotty youth wearing a pair of illuminated antlers is serving a large and sullen queue at Glasgow union convenor work-to-rule pace. This gives me time to survey the UK seasonal economy, and wonder at the resilience of the British consumer. One woman has a trolley full of Huggies nappies, kitchen wipes and Panadol. Another has a large bottle of cooking sherry and a toilet brush. The man in front has the bachelor Christmas special: a tin of frankfurters, a pot noodle, four tins of John Smiths bitter and the Readers' Wives Christmas Edition of *Men Only*. How depressing.

 Elevenses: A plain chocolate Bounty consumed while in the queue. I would have had time to finish a family pack, had I known.

Christmas Afternoon: Underwhelmed, Overground

Eunice was less than overwhelmed by my gifts: Natralox organic anti-wrinkle cream, three Budleigh Salterton tea towels, a new mat to go around the base of the loo, and a Jeffrey Archer omnibus.

"Bernard, you know I don't like Jeffrey Archer. I've never been to Budleigh Salterton, and do I need to be reminded I have the odd smile line?"

Grimace gorges, more like. Her gifts to me were equally disappointing. A set of points for the railway layout, new slippers and a computer programme that calculates your damn cholesterol. Oh, yes. A box of Maltesers too.

"Only one at a time, and only after meals, Bernard," she said.

Brian and Janet bought me John Train's biography of Warren Buffett, *The Midas Touch*, which looks excellent.

Digby had been more imaginative, thoughtfully vandalising one of my existing double-O passenger footbridges for a more post-Beeching feel.

"Look Grandad. I painted Man U and Spurs on the side, and some naughty 'F' words. And glued some tiny bits of broken glass on the stairs, just behind the hoodies, see there? They've just happy-slapped that commuter for his phone."

"Ah yes. Very realistic, very urban. What are these pink and orange splotches supposed to be?"

"That's puke."

Well, I can't complain that my railway does not fully capture the British travelling experience, I suppose.

Wednesday 26th December: The Day After

This morning I caught the Antichrist trying to wheedle money out of my mother. "Great Granny, I really wanted a bike this year, and Mum and Dad only got me some X-Box games."

"But you might fall off and hurt yourself, poppet," she responded, unaware of the sophisticated scheming taking place.

"But these have stabilisers." At which point Digby slipped on to her lap a quad bike brochure. "Look, these are really safe."

Dot of course, can't tell the difference between a quad bike and a child's tricycle and looked quite ready to break out the cash until I intercepted the malevolent mite. He's still only nine, but destined to become the dictator of some impoverished country. I just hope he'll remember his grandad when he's rich.

Thursday 27th December: Perfect Peter Boasts

Peter Edgington rings. As usual, he beat the market in 2007, having taken gains in May and stayed largely in cash for the rest of the year. This year, he tells me, he is tempted by gold and soft commodities, though he's steering clear of base metals and oils.

"My main conundrum is this," he tells me. "I am principally attracted to yield, whose reinvestment plays such a large part in historic returns. Yet the traditional income plays, such as banks and property, are either distressed or depressed so I'm not ready to buy yet. By contrast pure commodities or funds offer good price action, but little income. I'm just not comfortable relying on purely gainsaying the market for my return. It's too easy to be wrong."

What Olympian detachment Peter manages. I seem to spend most of the year trying to scramble out of various fixes that the market has dragged me into. Bovis, Domino's Pizza and QinetiQ come to mind. I never seem to find time to make a top-down asset or sectoral allocation. Maybe that's my problem. Plus having no money of course. Only £138 in the current account, and the inevitable mountainous Christmas credit card bill of Eunice's, due in a day or two. Time to work on my mother again, perhaps. If Digby can almost manage to wring some out of her for a damned quad bike, I should be able to.

Friday 28th December: Crossed Wires

Mightily relieved to take my mother back to Isleworth, to be rid of the vague smell of world war two cabbage that seems to surround her, and her continuing search for the clothing coupons she lost in 1947. My grievous grandchild didn't help, having dragged in Maurice, Dot's mobility vehicle, from the porch and raced up and down the hall doing Murray Walker voiceovers and making skidding noises. There is now a suspiciously large dent in the base of the grandfather clock.

So, finally on the M25 and with a captive audience, Dot regales me with the latest local scandal from the McCarthy & Stone sheltered housing complex opposite.

"Ida Tidworth's got a toyboy!"

"Oh, come on, she's older than you, isn't she?"

"Yes, 94 next birthday. She's always been a one, has Ida. She was the first in our street to sleep with a Yank, and that was before we couldn't get stockings. It was an investment, she said. And she was the first to have a hysterectomy, before they became all the rage."

"So how old is the toyboy?" I asked, my nausea at the idea not quite strong enough to overcome my curiosity.

"Young Jimmy? Not yet 76. Ida was head bridesmaid at his mother's wedding in 1929. Ooh, she's a dirty beggar. Still, he's only after her widow's pension. Ida's Percy was big in offal, you know, and they always had a good pension in offal. Plus all the kidney you could eat."

Saturday 29th December: Credit Crisis

Eunice's credit card bill duly arrives, ominously by parcel post. She's out shopping, would you believe, so I sit down pour myself a large Talisker, and break open this millstone of misery. Page after page. Wyevale £23.17, Argos £123.16, Debenhams £106.67, and Waitrose after Waitrose after Waitrose. The grand total, which doesn't yet include any of December, is a staggering £917.43. Really, it's time for a decision. Eunice arrives in time to find me with an air of purpose, loading the Volvo's roof rack.

"Bernard, what are you doing? Isn't that Brian's old canoe you have on top there?"

"That's right."

"If you're going to the hospice shop, I've got lots of other thing to take. Just give me a few minutes."

"I'm not going to the hospice shop. I'm off to Hartlepool, to do some coastal canoeing."

"What on earth are you talking about?"

"This is what I'm talking about," I say, brandishing the credit card bill. "You're living beyond my means, and I've exhausted every possibility to keep up. We're soon going to be up debt creek without a paddle. So I'm going to fake my own death and start a new life in Panama, or Xanadu or perhaps Kettering. You can claim on the life insurance, which should keep you in organic pulses, elasticated trousers and bunion protectors for a month or two. When the form comes write 'Cause of death: a broken wallet'."

"Bernard, don't be ridiculous. We're comfortably off, surely?"

"If you look at what we have in the house, it appears so, but scratch the surface and we're distinctly sub-prime. I mean, how is it that banks which have been so reluctant to lend to each other are happy to lend you £18.16 to spend at 'Just Candleholders' or £58.19 for an aromatherapy massage at Sensual Softies? That's reckless lending by any standard."

New Year's Eve: Treasure Trove

Well good riddance to 2007. Miserable market performance, no progress on getting my mother to begin some estate planning, and almost entirely deprived of spare cash by Eunice. If I were a share,

I'd certainly suffer from a demanding spouse-to-earning ratio. My attempt on Saturday to canoe myself into a different life (off sunny Hartlepool) was stymied by a bout of wifely tears. I was dragged inside, fed a placatory Malteser, and given a promise of more thoughtful spending in 2008. I'll believe that when it happens.

However, I then suffered the indignity of a let's-make-it-up hippopotamus manoeuvre on our poor sofa, which protested more loudly than a short-changed London cabbie, before finally breaking a spring. Still, in the ensuing repair mission I did find down the back a yellowed £10 Timothy Whites gift voucher (will Boots still honour it?) a collection of Portuguese escudos, and a half-eaten Penguin, which I will put aside for emergencies.

7.30pm. In a few minutes the harridans from Eunice's basket-weaving classes and the old girls of St Cecilia's will be arriving for an evening of post-menopausal mayhem to see the New Year in. I will, if possible, attempt to hide in the attic and install the new double 'O' points I received at Christmas. Certainly there is nothing in Eunice's planned buffet to tempt me to leave aside the painting of my signal box. I can do without wild mushroom pate, fennel flan and six bean casserole, thank you very much. Besides, in the layout's big tunnel I have secreted a box of Netto fig rolls, half a tin of Scottish shortbread and a Flake.

New Year's Day: Not The Party Type

What a performance! Last night's witches' party started raucous and got worse. Eunice, Chilean wine box in one hand and G&T in the other, made several intoxicated attempts to cajole me down to watch a video called *Hot Fuzz* with the assembled multitude. However, having overheard Angharad's voice booming from the kitchen for the last 15 minutes, I'm quite sure I know more than enough about bikini waxing as it is.

Back in the loft, I tuned-in on the portable black-and-white to see the New Year in, only to find a two-headed Geordie creature called Anton Deck was hogging the show, so instead went to bed by 12.05am with a small single malt. Sleep was impossible, and earplugs proved ineffective. Out in the garden, I could see drunken matrons cavorting around, with wine glasses in each hand while the hi-fi belted out "Women are doing it for themselves."

Well, I wish they bloody would and leave me alone.

Chapter Seven

New Year Resolutions

Wednesday 9th January 2008: Cosmetic Surgery

A bleary-eyed meeting at the Ring o'Bells. K.P. Sharma, the first to arrive, is in a bad mood. He shows me on his laptop the spreadsheets he has constructed for bank shareholdings.

"You know," he says. "I have laboriously entered all the assets and liabilities from the annual reports of four banks I own shares in. It took hours, but I wanted to be confident that I understood how the capital was deployed. But now I discover that conduits, SIVs and other whatnots are lurking outside. Contingent liabilities, you know, are the hardest of all threats to predict. Especially if you don't know the contingencies they relate to."

"But isn't there a proposal to create a secondary balance sheet to bring these liabilities into the light?" I responded.

"Look, Bernard. Regulators obviously want to unearth banking assets that they can then regulate and harness into capital ratios. Naturally, bankers want to hide assets where they can generate more profit on less capital. It doesn't matter what they call a secondary balance sheet, the urge to hide will remain."

Harry Staines lifts his eye from the pages of *The Daily Sport*. "Blimey, what are you two on about?" He tuts and points to the paper. "Look, here's a real investment theme for you. It says here that private medical spending has fallen so sharply that breast enlargement clinics in Harley Street have started doing special three for the price of two offers."

Unfortunately, K.P. falls for this anatomical impossibility, and leafs through in a vain quest for the article in question.

"Okay," says Harry. "Here's a real idea. We should short-sell every company the moment the boss gets a gong."

"Yeah," says Chantelle. "Sir Stuart Rose should be called Sir Stuart Fell after his effect on my M&S shares yesterday."

"I made this list," Harry says. "Sir Adrian Montagu at British Energy, and Sir John Ritblat of British Land got on their knees at the start of 2006 and the shares were on their knees within a year."

"What about Sir Philip Green?" Martin says.

"Except you can't get the shares," K.P. noted.

The afternoon brightens up considerably as we amass as many share charts as we can and match them to honours for a contrarian strategy. Perhaps pride comes before a share price fall?

Thursday 10th January: No Gain Without Pain

Miserable start to 2008. I think I have to make some new year resolutions and this time keep to them. First, I'm going to have to get to grips with stop-losses. Anything that falls 15% from today's price, I'm going to sell. Having seen the misery over house prices I'll start with Bovis. I bought this benighted investment for 660p in December 2005, after which it soared to 1200p in March. Why didn't I sell then? I have no idea. Everyone's been crying wolf about house price crashes for years, so that you just shrug it off. After all, house prices were still rising in the summer, so instead of selling when Bovis fell, I bought more at 920p instead of following a stop-loss. So now, shame-facedly, I really am going to sell, and I'm not going to wait for tomorrow's trading statement. What riches do I get for these shares? Just 490p. Appalling. Less than I began with, and little more than half what I paid for the latest tranche. What an exercise in self-flagellation!

 Elevenses: Misery loves company, so they say. That, I believe, was a mistranslation from the ancient Welsh. Misery is Celtic shorthand for Llanelli-Job-Centre-on-a-rainy-Monday-morning-in-November. What misery actually loves is confectionery. Find the fattest, most washed-out and most dejected face on any platform in the Southern Region, and you won't have to wait long before seeing a Mars Bar pushed into it. It is a well-known medical fact that you can't smile and consume chocolate simultaneously. Anyway, in honour of my own membership of the financial Hara Kiri brigade, I'm re-opening the Hornby drawer as of today, with a two-for-one packet of jaffa cakes, a mint chocolate Aero and enough shortbread to build a bailey bridge for the model railway. I shall defend it to the last from foreign spies.

Friday 11th January: Brake With Tradition

Recession looms in the U.S., sub-prime worries hitting big banks, shares falling, debt rising. Everyone, everywhere is putting the brakes on. Except Eunice.

For most of her driving life I've had to remind her to release the handbrake before driving off (anything to help fuel consumption). This time it appears she deigned not to use it at all. She was queuing up the hill to turn right out of Horsham Drive yesterday and let the car roll backwards into a brand new Saab. She's only had the new Clio six weeks, and now the limited edition back is stoved in, which makes it an even more limited edition, and there is an irate Saab-driving barrister threatening to have her banned. The damage to the Clio is at least £2000. Yet the only thing Eunice seems bothered about is the bruise on her eyelid.

"I can't believe it," Eunice said, looking in the mirror as I drove her home. "I'm beginning to look like Joe Bugner."

"Beginning?"

One stinging slap later, I admitted that there were significant differences between the two. One, Eunice had rarely been more than a welterweight. Two, she was much the better fighter.

"Bernard, you don't possess a scintilla of human sympathy."

"Look. If you hadn't been applying mascara at a junction you wouldn't have got the brush in your eye, would you?

"I could have the lost sight in one eye!"

"Well, that would be one eye's improvement on how you currently drive."

Sunday 13th January: Money Laundering

Round to see my lunatic mother. Her washing machine is playing up. She says the clothes are coming out dirty. She is correct in this, but that is not the whole truth. In fact they are coming out exactly the way they went in, unwashed and dry. The inlet hose is blocked with lint. While I sort this out, I can't help noticing a pile of letters on top of the fridge. Included among them is a year-end statement from her stockbroker, which I quickly stuff into my overalls. At least I can see how my inheritance is performing.

Monday 14th January: Bailiff Time

Disturbed by a hammering on the door at 8.45am. Go down in my dressing gown to see a large and unapologetic Scottish woman who claims to be from Wormald and Scrivens, the bailiff.

"Is your wife in?" she says, waving a piece of pink paper.

Across the road I could see Daphne Hanson-Hart watching closely, having seen the van. The Jones stock is clearly falling in Endsleigh Gardens.

"It's not about her credit card, is it?" I ask.

"Aye. And the Barclayloan, the secured loan, the unapproved overdraft and the failure to stick to the previous agreement to repay £26,000 in arrears that we agreed with her two years ago."

Suddenly I felt my world begin to fall apart. I know Eunice had been a little free and easy with my money, but this was just a shock greater than anything I had ever experienced. I couldn't believe that Eunice had got us into enough debt to require a bailiff. How had she done it without me noticing?

"So anyway," said the female bailiff. "Your wife has seven days to make a substantial cash payment on these accounts or we get a warrant from the court, Mr O'Riordan."

O'Riordan? Aha! O'Riordan!

"I think you have the wrong address. The O'Riordan's live there," I said, pointing to the lime green front door just visible behind the giant camper van parked on the grass verge. "We are Mr and Mrs Bernard Jones."

The bailiff apologised profusely. Much relieved, I walked upstairs, and encountered Eunice drying herself after a shower.

"What was all that?" she said.

"Nothing to worry your pretty head about," I said kissing her on the tip of the nose. "Would you like to go out to dinner tonight? I'm paying."

The look she gave me was of extreme shock.

Wednesday 16th January: Trauma At The Bar

The scheduled share club meeting turns out to be inquorate. K.P. Sharma gave his apologies, according to a message from Chantelle, who today is on kitchen duty. No Martin Gale, no Mike Delaney. Harry Staines, though present, is in no condition to invest in anything more complex than a fifth pint of Hambledon Nightmare. It seems to be one of the immutable laws of investing that when the markets are miserable, you can't get anyone interested. Yet surely we should either be bargain hunting or selling losers. I'm not sure which, but at least I'm here to discuss it. While I'm considering what to do Mr Abrasive himself, Russell Traugh, sidles up to me at the bar.

"How much has your share club lost this year then?" he asks, with a carious grin. "'Cos I'm still in the money."

"Oh yes?" I say, trying not to encourage him.

He leans over conspiratorially, and I get a whiff of pickled onion tainted BO. "That Ukrainian farm company, Landkom, is up 15% from where I bought it in November. They've already got their first crop planted, ready to harvest in July. I'm going to make a fortune from that one, you mark my words. I'm doing well with Corin, Dignity and Genus too.

"Very good. Well done," I say, trying to get away.

"Your share club will never make a bean if they don't take it seriously," he says. "I mean, look at him." He points to Harry's recumbent form, propped in front of the pub TV where Wallace and Gromit is showing. "How's he ever going to make a penny? Any profits he has he drinks," Russell whispers.

"Well there's no danger of you spending yours at the bar," is there Russ?" Harry growls. "You're tighter than Elvis's Y-fronts."

Thursday 17th January: Retail Therapy Needed

Under a heap of papers in the den I rediscover my mother's 2007 portfolio summary, which I snitched earlier this week. This account looked clever enough in the summer, when Mary Asterby at the Women's Institute helped her reshape it. The £150,000 that Dot gave to my errant daughter Jemima in August seemed to come from the sale of gilts, which looks wholly the wrong decision because it left the rest of the portfolio, almost solely retailers, looking very shabby indeed. The latest prices make grim reading: Laura Ashley, down 17% since July; Marks & Spencer and British Airways, each down 40%, Carnival Cruise Line, down 27%, Care UK down 48%. Even artificial hip joint maker Smith & Nephew is down 5%. Only funeral directors Dignity is up. What was a £690,000 portfolio in July is now worth just £410,000, little short of a disaster. I ring my mother, and ask her what she plans to do about her investments.

"What investments, Bernard?" she responds

"Your shares. You have hundreds of thousands of pounds tied up in shares that are going down."

"No I don't. My money's in the Post Office. Anyway, going down where?

"Look, Mum, you have a portfolio at the stockbrokers, don't you? You know, Marks & Spencer and British Airways? Shares traded on the stock market. And prices are falling very fast."

"Ooh, has Marks got a sale on then? I could do with a new cardy. This one's starting to pill on the sleeves. Still, that's British Home Stores for you, they never quite had the quality"

"Mum, please listen. This isn't about shopping, it's about your savings. If you don't believe me call Mary Asterby of the WI, she'll explain it to you. Only please do something, because you are losing thousands of pounds every day."

Friday 18ᵗʰ January: Severe Handbagging

The FTSE plunged below 5600 this morning. Suddenly feel a little nervous about my mother's retail-heavy portfolio. Rang Mary Asterby, Dot's investment guru from the WI. After receiving five minutes of severe hectoring I wish I hadn't bothered.

"Well really, Mr Jones. I really don't think it is any business of yours how your mother's investments are arranged. She came to us because you were bullying her, and now you are at it again."

"Look, what you did was very good initially, I'll admit that," I said. "You got her to spread her investments over a wide range of shares, but you just overdid it on the retailers. The portfolio has underperformed the FTSE 100 by 10% since the summer."

"How would you know, Mr Jones? I'm not aware you are privy to the current constituents of the portfolio."

"Er...no. I just assumed that what was in it in July is still in it."

"Let me tell you something, Mr Jones. The Knott's Green WI share club, of which I am the chair, has outperformed the FTSE All-share by an average 2% every year since inception in 1957. We know what we are doing. I have taken your mother under my wing, and I will look after her. Your self-serving 'help' is not appreciated. Are we perfectly clear?"

 Elevenses: After that I needed a jaffa cake, six squares of Aero and a shortbread to recover.

Saturday 19ᵗʰ January: Hippopotamuses Manoeuvring

Had a nightmare about being charged by a herd of hippopotamus wearing fishnet tights and fluffy slippers. Awake in panic from this horrific vision, and then realise what my unconscious is trying to tell me. There really is a herd on the way! Our anniversary is on the 29th, Eunice's birthday, Feb 4th (I wonder if Harland and Wolff have a plaque commemorating their most durable dreadnought) and then Valentine's Day itself. I thought that as the years wore on (and my lower vertebrae wore out) the physical act would gradually be consigned to the cupboard of our marriage along with the silly love letters and noisome endearments. Not a bit of it. Led on by Irmgard, that rabid feminist, Eunice is demanding that I spend valuable railway modelling time exploring obscure new erogenous zones. There are apparently such a profusion of them (are they downloadable from the Internet?) that they now denote them just with letters. Now we're up to 'G' and this one's so tiny it is just called a 'spot'. Unable to find it so far. I suspect it's lurking near a mini-roundabout in West Bromwich. It's certainly not on my 1988 AA road atlas. Perhaps they have directions on satnav?

Sunday 20th January: Tax Demands

Oh God, Oh God. I've forgotten to do my tax return and it has to be with them, plus the money, by the end of the month. Can't find the damn form anywhere. Perhaps the easiest thing would be to do it online. I know I did sign up last year and didn't use it. Cannot find the password anywhere. Phone up the help desk, spent a long while waiting listening to bloody Vivaldi, finally got through. With new password I get online, but the little wavy Windows flag thingy on Internet Explorer just waves and nothing happens. After half an hour I ring up again. More Vivaldi. Finally I get to speak to someone. The website's apparently busy. Well, there's a surprise at the height of tax panic season. There's no planning is there? It's just like going to the damn Post Office at lunchtime. Finally at 11.17pm, six hours later, I finish inputting my meagre figures. The resultant bill is £1430.16, less than I'd feared but still unaffordable.

There's only one thing for it. Instead of paying for Eunice's credit card bill with cash, I'll use the cash in my account to settle the tax bill, and pay Eunice's Barclaycard bill with one of those cunning but dangerous credit card cheques I got with my gold card. It's a cash advance that looks like proper money, and the start of a very slippery slope. I hope I don't end up like Martin Gale, running round in ever decreasing financial circles with only an IVA to look forward to. Finally get to bed at 2.15am, waking Eunice.

"Bernard, where on earth have you been? It's gone two."

"Doing our taxes."

"I thought you did them before."

"Clearly not. We have a major financial crisis."

"Really?" she yawned. "I hope you've not been investing in odd loans like that Beryl Lynch," she yawned.

"It's Merrill not Beryl and no I haven't. Perhaps if you invested in fewer cars or didn't crash them so often we'd be okay."

"What about you? Spending our pension money drinking at the Ring o'Bells and frittering away on shares the cash that we could put in the Halifax." Eunice adjusted her eye mask, reinserted her earplugs and switched out the light. End of conversation.

There you have it. The meeting of minds that is a marriage.

Chapter Eight

Chinese Ordeal

Monday 21st January: Tanking Shares

Unbelievably grim morning in the market. No one really has a clue what's going on. There is all sorts of talk about the emerging markets no longer being able to decouple. It had never seemed likely to me that they could. FTSE is under 5400. There won't be any guidance from Wall Street because it's closed for Martin Luther King Day. Martin Gale phones me to ask what we should do. I don't know. Chantelle rings and asks the same. No one can get hold of K.P. Sharma. Reluctantly, I ring Peter Edgington who was blissfully unaware of all the shenanigans.

"I really shouldn't panic, Bernard," he tells me. "I presume by now you have plenty of your portfolio in cash?"

"Well, I sold all my shares in Bovis. But most of the money I raised I used to settle the excess on Eunice's car prang and some of the stuff that wasn't covered in the so-called comprehensive cover. I've probably got £400 spare."

"Goodness me, Bernard. I had no idea you invested on such a shoestring. Haven't you had any luck with your mother's holdings? I thought she was quite wealthy."

"Don't get me started on that, Peter. She's being totally obtuse. I'm sure she'll eventually leave the whole lot to a refuge for incontinent badgers in Ormskirk."

'Perfect' Peter is so casually superior, and so unconcerned by the market that I get very irritated. Do we not inhabit the same planet? I return to Lemon Curdistan to fret and to eat.

 Elevenses: Half a bar of Aero and two jaffa cakes.

5pm. Hear that Jeremy Paxman has the same trouble with M&S underwear as I have. His gusset gripe earns him a meal with Stuart Rose, whereas my complaint about those bloody ridiculous tartan boxer shorts that Jem got me a couple of Christmases ago earned me nothing but sarcasm and derision.

Tuesday 22nd January: Dungeons And Dragons

Martin Gale rings at 8.15am to let me know what I can already see: that the market is dropping like a stone again. Definitely panicking, he wants the share club to sell everything immediately.

"But look, Martin, we might already be near the bottom."

"I don't think so. I was looking at these charts in *Chronic Investor* magazine, and they reckon the FTSE may hit 4900."

I manage to dissuade him from trying to arrange an emergency share club meeting. Once he is gone I look at my own shares, expecting carnage. Actually, it's not too bad. QinetiQ, Compass and Domino's Pizza are all steady to improving. Hornby is miserable, but fortunately I don't have many. Lloyds TSB is depressed, but at least I can look forward to a big dividend. However, the one thing which really enrages me is Bovis. This benighted house builder, which I sold at 490p earlier this month has jumped to 600p. Isn't there supposed to be a housing crisis on? Falling prices, loan problems? The indebted British consumer? Looks like the market professionals just wait for all the country's amateur Bernards to capitulate and then they buy. I feel cheated.

At this moment Eunice pads in eating toast and jam. She is draped in a pink housecoat, has rollers in her hair and a hideous orange varnish on her toenails.

"And how are things in the hallowed halls of high finance?" she smirks, leaning over to look at the screen while dropping blobs of greengage jam into the keyboard of the PC.

"Well, not too bad," I say, looking her up and down. "And how are things in the London Dungeon?"

I cringe for the clout that never comes. Eunice's mind is instead on high culture.

"Don't forget, Bernard. We're going to see a show tonight."

"What? I don't remember this."

"Yes you *do*. In told you in October. We've got tickets for Qing Wao Tsao at Tunbridge Wells with Irmgard and Nils.

"Oh how absolutely thrilling," I murmur. "What is it?"

"It's a rustic Chinese opera about Mao's long march in 1934. It got absolutely rave reviews in *Time Out*."

"So did picketing Grunwick, gay rights and comprehensive schooling. Now look at the state the country's in."

"Bernard, really. You'd make Mussolini seem progressive."

Wednesday 23rd January: Oriental Ordeal

2am. This cannot wait until the morning. Just back from four hours of torture at the so-called Chinese opera. The programme (£3 a copy!) described it as '...a poignant loss of rural innocence, set against a backdrop of proletarian struggle.' The proletarian struggle in question was presumably to afford the £40 cost per ticket plus five quid booking fee. The 'singing' was more like a warm-up for national cat-strangling week. No wonder China's economy is booming, taking us westerners for suckers at every turn.

8.45am. Get up this morning to find that the Fed cut rates by three-quarters of a point to 3.5% yesterday, and the markets have rallied strongly. This is clearly strong medicine, but I don't really see how it will help. The global economy has overdone it on cheap loans, and has awoken with a paralysing credit hangover. However cheap the Fed makes borrowing, it won't want to glug any more down for a while. Just as with alcohol, it's time, not extra imbibing, that will restore health. It does, however, show that the Greenspan 'put' is alive and well in the days of Bernanke. Inflation worries, it seems, can go hang. Speaking of which, my MoD pension payment has cleared and I can am flush for a week or two.

At share club, we have a full house.

"So is it all over then?" Martin Gale asks.

"I think it's barely begun," K.P. Sharma says. "There is supposed to be a European bank in trouble."

Chantelle, today in ripped and re-stitched mini-skirt, black eye shadow and black spider-web tights, says the metals market is sagging. Her father, a scrap metal dealer, is not getting the price for copper he was three months ago, though lead is still going well.

"Which church roof is he off to strip today?" asks Harry.

"He isn't like that, " she retorts. "You're just prejudiced!"

"Perhaps Harry is suffering from ferroemporiphobia," I suggest. "Fear of those who trade iron."

With our accumulated dues we now have £2000 to spend, but we agree to keep it in cash until prices have fallen further.

Thursday 24th January: Derivative Dingbat

France's *Société Générale* has come a €5 billion cropper this morning in a rogue trader scandal. Using managers' passwords, false-hedges and delayed margin calls this financial Spiderman has apparently woven a clever web for his employers to struggle in. Just one skill missing though: an ability to make money from it.

My tyrant grandson Digby will undoubtedly aspire to this one day, with his malevolent intelligence and cunning. I taught him to play chess last weekend. By the third game he was beating me, and by the fourth giving me advice. He may still be nine, but I can see him in fifty years time sitting in a winged armchair stroking a cat and plotted the destruction of global civilisation.

 Elevenses: No matter that the border of Lemon Curdistan is officially closed, Eunice mounts an incursion armed with rubber gloves while I am eating the last of my Aero.

"Excuse me. The sign says 'do not disturb'," I say.

"Bernard, I've come to do the windows. They're as filthy as you are," Eunice retorts, pushing past me with a J-cloth in one hand and a Windolene spray in the other. She dumps Prescott the suede pig on my lap, shoves aside a pile of annual reports, and clambers onto the desk to open the window.

"For goodness sake woman, everything's blowing around!"

"I'm sorry, but I will not put up with this mess anymore," she says. "Look at the crumbs everywhere, the coffee rings, the old cake wrappers behind the desk which you think I can't see. Didn't you read that research which found more germs on workplace desks than on toilet seats? Now call me picky, but I don't want to be blamed for Endsleigh Gardens' first outbreak of ebola."

After finishing scrubbing at the windows, she laid into the PC screen, squirting Windolene on it and scrubbing it vigorously. Finally she turned to face me. "Give me those," she said, pointing to my reading glasses.

"Oh for goodness sake. Why can't you leave me alone?"

"Bernard, they're filthy and you can't possibly see a thing." She reaches out, I dodge and then get sprayed in the eyes.

"Aaarggh!" I squeal, quite reasonably.

"Stop fussing. None of this would have happened if you'd stayed still. Don't be a cry-baby".

I crawl on hands and knees to the bathroom, where I rinse the damn stuff out of my eyes and wonder where the nearest refuge for battered investors is.

Saturday 26th January: Checkmate

Brian has some function at school, and he and Janet have dumped the Antichrist with us for the day. Entertaining this rude child was never easy, but in chess I at least thought I had an answer. Nevertheless, after eight minutes this mini-master is a queen, a knight and a battalion of pawns ahead and complains he is bored. Between moves, he either fiddles with his mobile phone or yawns loudly. I've an idea. I'll get him to play Perfect Peter. Peter is in a chess club, I believe. That should be a good challenge. Besides, whoever loses, somebody who richly deserves it will be taken down a peg or two.

Monday 28th January: Profits Hit The Buffers

Hornby's results today a little disappointing. Delays in delivering new products into the European market are expected to hit profits by £1 million. A little alarmed to see that hefty inflation-busting price increases are being planned. What was the point of moving to China if costs don't come down? In any case, I might race down and get that new set of coal trucks before the rise takes effect.

Elevenses: A Crunchie bar. I don't know whether it is a phoney war or not, but there has been no trace of Eunice nosing through the Hornby drawer for months now. Instead, she seems to be rearranging our bedroom. There have been some very loud thumping and banging noises, and she later emerges with a flushed face. I dread to think what she is doing up there.

Wednesday 30th January: Anniversary Antics

Eunice has booked a room at Boarfield Priory, a five star hotel on the Weald which also boasts a haunted cellar. Perhaps she is hoping to commune with some of her more eccentric ancestors. Great aunt Gladys, for example, was known as Glad the Impaler after her dreaded soirées in which every known food (and a few unknown ones) were served on cocktail sticks. Then there was uncle Horace, who had six P&O steamer trunks (later discovered to be stuffed with *Health & Efficiency* magazines), but whose only boating experience was crossing Tooting Bec Lido in a pedalo.

We arrive to find the room is excellent and, courtesy of winter rates, not too expensive. After a first rate meal and a bottle of excellent Barolo, we follow with port. Eunice is now, as she describes it 'squiffy' and that undoubtedly means the hippos are being marshalled for manoeuvre. In the bedroom, I get into bed and feign (indeed, would now embrace) death, while Eunice takes two bulging carrier bags into the bathroom. I am genuinely asleep by the time she emerges, but as thirteen stone of spouse crashes onto the bed it is the squeal of PVC that truly frightens me. Pinioned beneath the covers, I look up to see what appears to be a crimson blancmange unbuttoning my pyjama top. With apparitions like this to haunt you, who needs ghosts? Next I am turfed out of my pyjama bottoms. This process is conducted with all the gentleness of a Mount Pleasant shop steward emptying mailbags at the end of an unofficial strike. Eunice doesn't remove her plasticised ensemble, but from the squealing and creaking, it seems close to making its own decision. A cold arm then snakes beneath the covers for five minutes of clumsy fumbling and groping. Eventually, Eunice sticks her head under the covers and declares: "Is that the best you can do? Oh come on Bernard, make an effort."

"But it's late and I'm tired."

"It's our *anniversary*. It really isn't too much to ask, is it, that a wife can expect her husband to make love to her on the day which celebrates their marriage?"

"I'm sorry, I really am trying, for your sake. But it's a quarter to two, I'm dog tired and I've had three glasses of wine and a port."

"Well, I've had four glasses, two G&Ts, and a port, and I'm more than ready."

"But you're *always* more than ready, regardless of circumstances. Anyway, everyone knows alcohol has the opposite effect on women than on men."

"Well, you shouldn't have drunk so much then, if you knew it was going to inhibit your erection. You have this problem time and again, and won't do anything about it."

"The only problem I have is trying to get my fair share of a bottle of Barolo," I retorted.

"And another thing. I make a huge effort to arouse you, and you do absolutely nothing to reciprocate. I mean I've got a new outfit, I wear stockings which is what I read that men always find sexy, but there you are in a pair of worn-out British Home Stores pyjamas that you've had since the Reformation. I give up, really I do."

Well, thank God for that.

Monday 4th February: Generations Apart

Eunice is 60 today. I have, as requested, bought her a green leotard (Size 16, Age Concern £2!) "Look, I'm the Green Goddess," she says, with a twirl that threatens to send acres of mottled cellulite into orbit.

"Well, you'll certainly be a great help if the fire brigade goes out on strike again," I reply.

Eunice is distracted from considering my reply by the arrival of a four-foot long parcel. While I sip my coffee, she tears apart the packaging to reveal a series of metal tubes.

"Oh. Decided to retrain as a scaffolder?" I ask.

"No, Bernard. I'm going to pole dance my way to fitness."

"You're going to *what*?"

"It's the 'in' thing. All the moves that these burlesque dancers do are the perfect way to achieve true fitness. I want to sculpt by body back to youthful perfection. Look, here's the DVD which shows you how to do it."

"Eunice, dearest," I say in my softest tones. "You are 60 today. Not sixteen. Perhaps something a little less demanding?"

"Bernard, I sometimes think you'd like me to be gradually embalmed in sweet sherry in front of the test card, like your mother. You may be resigned to slipping into a cardigan-shrouded old age, but I am not. I read an article in the *Mail* the other day that a non-smoking woman of my age can expect to live until she's almost 90. That's another 50% more life than I've lived already. I'm determined to do it with style. We're at peace, aren't we? We can afford to travel the world and we have our health. We shouldn't squander our good luck! I shall lose two stone in the next two months. Once I am trim again, believe me, I shall turn heads."

Turn heads? Probably not. Stomachs, certainly. It's all very well to live life to the full, but that costs money and our pension arrangements are stretched funding a frugal old age, the odd cruise to the Canaries, new cane furniture for the conservatory and motoring holidays in the Dordogne. The bewhiskered actuaries at Norwich Union would be appalled to see that the nation's thin gruel of with-profits and annuity income is actually being used by over-ambitious matrons to fund Raymond Revue Bar callisthenics, Caribbean paragliding lessons and scuba-diving adventures.

"So was this what all this grunting and banging upstairs was about? Were you doing exercises?"

"Yes. I'm strengthening my pelvic floor."

"If I were you, I'd concentrate on strengthening the bedroom floor first. We don't want it to turn this into a trapeze show on the dining room light fitting do we?"

Chapter Nine

A Tough Delivery

Friday 8ᵗʰ February: BHP Not High Enough

The share club's one successful pick, mining company BHP Billiton, has today been labelled as 'high enough' by *Chronic Investor* magazine. High enough? Not for us. It was 1900p a few months back, and is only 1650p now. Given China's hunger for metals that's surely not nearly high enough. We bought it for 1155p back in 2006, and are hoping for a crisp twenty quid.

Elevenses: Two jaffa cakes while waiting in for a delivery. I ordered Eunice a Valentine's Day gift online, a book originally published in 1896, called *A Gentlewife's Guide To Pleasing Her Spouse*, by Lady Lucinder Mockett. I hope it might rebalance Eunice's views on the purpose of marriage. There is plenty about hiring domestic staff, arranging tissue paper when packing suitcases, and the correct way to iron spats. The nearest it has to coverage of sexual congress is an instruction of how to faint in style upon discovery of a gentleman's 'disarrayed cummerbund'.

5pm. No sign of the delivery. Damn!

Tuesday 12ᵗʰ February: Car Chase

Still no sign of that book. Rang the publisher who said a copy would definitely arrive tomorrow. Ten minutes later, just as I was getting the car out of the garage to go to the Ring o'Bells, I saw a City Link delivery van pulling away from the front of the house. I rushed back inside to find a note saying they had been 'unable to deliver a package because there was no reply'! I leapt into the car, and squealed out of the drive like Kojak heading for a wig fitting. The van was still in sight at the junction, but pulled out into the main road as I arrived. I tailed the vehicle for five miles, during which time it shot two sets of lights on amber, drove half on the pavement to avoid giving way to a cyclist and scattered two pram-pushing mums from a zebra crossing. Flashing my lights had no effect, but I finally cornered it at a council estate. The driver, a skinny youth who looked about 12 and had a Bluetooth earpiece, looked at me as if intended to rob him.

"Excuse me, I believe you have a parcel for me."

"S'number?"

"Number 17, Endsleigh Gardens."

"No mate, the delivery number of the package, like."

"How should I know? You haven't bloody delivered it. How can I give…?"

"It's on the card. The one I put 'froo the door."

"I haven't got that, I left it behind trying to catch you. Look. The parcel is for my wife, Eunice Jones of number 17…"

"Sorry mate. Phone the depot, and we'll deliver it tomorrow."

"But it's here in this van, right now! I can save you a journey."

"Sorry mate. I can't give you a package addressed to someone else. It's data protection, like."

"But you'd do it at the door!" I bellowed.

"Ah yes, but then we know that's the address n'all."

"But I've already TOLD YOU the address. Okay, here's proof," I fumbled in my pocket for my wallet, and eventually found my video hire card.

"Sorry mate. I can't do deliveries in the street."

"But I've just shown you my address!"

"It's not proof. You could just have mugged someone."

"How would I know that there was a parcel?"

"Now, if you had the card, it might be different," he said.

"How? I could still have mugged someone!"

"Yeah, but you'd have the delivery number."

"So it's alright to mug someone so long as you get the bloody delivery number, is it?" I shouted.

"Now you've adopted a threatening attitude. We can't deliver to customers who adopt a threatening attitude," the youth said.

"But you've already refused to deliver to me!"

"Keep your hair on, mate. We'll deliver it tomorrow."

Absolutely fuming, I returned to my car while the van containing Eunice's parcel pulled away to continue its mystery tour of Kent.

Wednesday 13th February: Failure To Deliver

Notice that Domino's Pizza has recovered quite well to 220p after the scare about the cheese price which hit it in November. To my view this is a stock that should do well in recessionary times. Britons now spend more on getting others to cook for us than we do on food we prepare ourselves, and Domino's represents the most affordable end of this marketplace.

Speaking of deliveries, by the time I go off to share club, there is still no sign of the damn parcel. I look up City Link's website and discover it is part of Rentokil. This is adding insult to injury! I had a painful share foray into that company's shares in 1998, which ended in loss-making ignominy in the market bubble of 2000. As far as I'm concerned Rentokil never seems to be able to deliver.

Thursday 14ᵗʰ February: Rentokilled

9.30am. It is now Valentine's Day and the book for Eunice has still not arrived. She's doing some last minute grocery shopping (for God-knows-what reason, as we're eating out tonight) and I'm twitching the curtains like Thora Hird waiting for the green and yellow City Link van that I was faithfully promised would be here.

 Elevenses: Two jaffa cakes, no book.

11.45am. Try to phone City Link, which must surely be the worst performing part of the Rentokil empire. Nonsensical automated voicemail system. After two minutes keying in my inside leg measurement or something, I slam the phone down in disgust and walk into the hall. There, on the doormat, is a delivery card: 'We called but you were out.' In the middle of my fury (akin to something tested on Christmas Island in 1957) the doorbell rings. I snatch up the nearest weapon, Jemima's pink polka-dot umbrella, and just pray that it is a Rentokil employee, who I intend to dispatch with Ninja-like efficiency.

I open the door to see Eunice, laden with bags, and presumably unable to find her key. "Bernard, What are you doing with that? It isn't raining, you know."

"I'm premeditating murder," I say, as I help with the bags.

"On Valentine's Day too, you old romantic! What did I do?"

I explain about the parcel and get a sympathetic hearing.

7.30pm. Dinner at a trendy Greek restaurant in the West End, recommended to us by Irmgard and Nils. Highlights were getting olive oil on my best blazer, a piece of kleftiko bone which chipped a filling, and a whopping great bill which included a hitherto undisclosed £6.75 per head 'cover charge'. While paying I offered my hope that as well as covering the cost of the stale pitta bread and teaspoon of humous and olives served, this would be put toward the cost of a course in civility for the waiting staff. While the manager scowled, Eunice told him to ignore me because I was going through the 'male menopause.'

11pm. Eunice had already had four big glasses of Chablis, but insisted we dip into the Duke of Abercrumble, or whatever, next door for a 'nightcap'. The noise hit us like a wall, the moment the door was opened. Like many West End pubs, it was festooned with signed black and white pictures of old time theatrical alcoholics. Peering at this legion of the forgotten and the forgettable, who had undoubtedly never visited this hostelry or at least never remembered, I marvelled they still had the nous to write "To my dearest landlady Violet" and other such tosh. Hacking my way to the bar, through thousands of baffled looking Korean tourists drinking half pints of Guinness, I reached an immovable obstacle: a ruck of bullet-headed South Africans in rugby shirts, none less than six feet tall, and in deafening good humour. Attracting the attention of the only barmaid, a dull-eyed Estonian stick insect of sullen countenance, proved quite impossible from this scrum half position, so I was forced to insinuate myself into the sweaty canyon between two gigantic voortrekkers.

"Hey, man. What about an 'igscuse me'," boomed one, as I nudged my way under his armpit.

"I've been saying nothing else for five minutes," I responded. "I even tapped you on the back, but all you did was scratch it."

"Just thought I'd got a gogga bug on me shoulder," he laughed "Tell ya what, tell me what you want and I'll order."

I told him we wanted a small whisky and ginger and a brandy. "Ach, bra, they're all small here. Still, let's get you fixed up right." He leaned over the bar, grabbed the barmaid by the shoulder and shouted something in her ear. He then took my twenty and passed it over the bar. The glasses passed back to me were full. "That's a double Courvoisier for your lady wife and this is for you, it's bladdy lekker."

"Look, that's very kind but I just wanted..."

"Here's your change, man." He gave me a fiver and a few coppers.

"Is that it? For two drinks?" I exclaimed.

"Ya, London's ixpensive, isn't it?" he said, and turned away.

At times like this, you have a simple choice. Either stand on principle and get your face re-arranged, or learn to like whatever it was you've been given. I took a sip of mine, which wasn't Scotch, but was quite tasty and handed Eunice her brandy.

"It's Courvoisier," I said. "A double."

"Ooh, Bernard. Are you trying to get me squiffy?" Eunice said, batted her eyelids at me in a highly unsubtle fashion.

"Trying? It's stopping you that would be the achievement."

It took me half an hour to steer a giggly Eunice back to the hotel. It was one of those supposedly genteel places just off Russell Square which charge £150 a night, but in fact wouldn't rate much above a B&B in Birmingham or Blackpool. Squeaky taps, hair still clogging the plughole, and (I'm pretty sure) a cockroach in the seal of the mini-bar. Feeling sober and broke, I started cleaning my teeth, knowing that a Valentine's Day hippopotamus manoeuvre was, barring miracles, only a few minutes away.

When I returned to the bedroom, Eunice was sprawled on the bed wearing, or let us more accurately say 'largely contained within', a French maid's outfit. "Ooh. M'sieur. I sink I forgot to clean ze room. How can I, 'ow you say, apologise? I promise I'll do any sink you want, "she slurred in her best *'Allo 'Allo* accent.

"Well, that's handy because there is indeed plenty of grime around the hand basin. And I'm afraid I found a toenail clipping on the cistern..."

"Oh, Bernard. Keep up the make-believe. Don't be a misery," Eunice pouted. "Alright, come here. Tell me your fantasies."

"Well, I'm not sure you want..."

"Come on, I'm open minded. It's Valentine's Day and I really don't care how dirty it is."

"Well, what I really like to imagine is,"

"Yes?"

"I imagine I'm in an enormous room, with dappled sunlight filtering through a skylight. There's a little smoke in the air, and a gentle vibration in the distance. Finally, there's a gentle ringing of bells as the 4.13 Great Western Express from Bristol Temple Meads crosses the beautifully constructed box-girder bridge in perfect double 'O' scale..."

"Bernard! Not *that* kind of fantasy. You know...sexual."

"I'm long past those, I'm afraid."

"No you're not..."

"I *am*."

"So what was it you were thinking about doing with that au pair, then?"

"With Astrid? What do you mean?"

"Don't try that innocent look with me. When you were a peeping Tom on her nude sunbathing in the O'Riordan's garden. Were you anticipating discussing the latest Hornby accessories?"

"I did *not* peep. I was repairing the light, and I fell."

"Nonsense. You're a voyeur and you well know it!"

"I am not. I happened to casually glance..."

"Bernard, you need the spinal flexibility of an anaconda to see out of that skylight. You did not glance, you risked your life on a rickety stool so that you could ogle like an old pervert. I wouldn't mind so much, but you never ogle me. You don't even...look. It's as if I don't exist for you," Eunice sobbed.

And so with sheer inevitability, another Valentine's Day, all expense and expectation, collapses into a furious row. This is so frustrating. We could have had a perfectly sensible and pleasant evening, like the rest of the grey generation, eating a quiet meal with a glass of wine. Then we could stroll back to our hotel room at 10pm to watch a film, or even repeats of *Last of the Summer Wine*. But no, Eunice constantly attempts to rekindle the fires of teenage passion from cold ashes that, in my case, were long ago swept up and dumped into the green recycling bin of our marriage.

Monday 18th February: Pole Vaulting

I've been whiling away the hours waiting for the damn parcel by looking up Rentokil Initial's annual report. What a rambling collection of businesses this is. Everything from rat poison to washroom servicing, interior plant landscaping, and in Asia "E-security". I'd love to short-sell the shares, but my spread-betting account is moribund and bereft of cash for margin. Besides, it really didn't work when I did the same with Marks & Spencer, I just succeeded in losing hundreds of pounds.

Elevenses: I had been hoping for the alleged re-delivery before midday, but by the time I allow myself an eccles cake, there is no sign of City Link. There is however some banging coming from the dining room. Once I have swallowed my tuck, I wander in to see Eunice on her hands and knees, with the contents of her pole dancing package laid out on the floor.

"I said I'd assemble that for you, dear."

"Yes, you also said in 1983 you would re-grout the kitchen tiles and in 2001 you solemnly promised to re-paper our bedroom. This, at least, I can do myself," Eunice replies.

"Yes, dear." I retreat to the den and try to ignore the clangs and grunts. When I return in half an hour Eunice is nowhere to be seen, but the pole is up. Indeed, so far up that the tightly braced floor and ceiling plates have cracked the delicate plaster above.

"For God's sake woman," I mutter as I try to ease the tension. However, I've only slackened a half-inch when the bottom half of the pole falls out of its sleeve with a ding, while above a chunk of plaster the size of a dustbin lid cracks away. The only thing stopping a ceiling collapse is the top half of the pole, which I am holding as firmly as I can.

Just then the doorbell rings. Damn! My parcel. Unable to leave my post, I yell for Eunice. No reply. I yell louder. No reply. "Just coming," I bellow towards the door. As I plead and curse, a card is, with agonising slowness, pushed through the letterbox. Two minutes later I hear the loo flush, and Eunice breezes downstairs in her green leotard.

"Bernard, what was all that shouting? There's no peace in this house…Oh God, what on earth have you done?"

"ME? You think I did THIS?" I bellow, and in that momentary twitch of rage the entire ceiling comes down.

Tuesday 19th February: Getting Up

Arrived with Eunice's morning cup of tea to find her distinctly grumpy. Even the cat, which has a far more secure place in her affections than I do, was unceremoniously pushed off the bed when she jumped on for her morning stroking session. Cleary, yours truly was going to be in for a much rougher experience. As usual I needed to reshuffle various objects on Eunice's bedside table to make way for the mug. Today it's worse than usual: earplugs, eye mask, tablets, nail clippers, nail file and emery board, plus a nine-item receipt from Boots. With my hands now being scalded by the hot mug, I place the mug on the receipt, about the only place it has room to go, and get a particularly severe tut from her.

"Bernard, don't leave a ring on that. I've got to take the gel-filled heel pads back today. No, not there. Not on the book. You know it leaves a heat mark!"

"But it's hot! I'm being burned." I lift the mug again.

"Oh don't be such a nancy-boy, Bernard. Hold on a minute."

While my knuckles are being gradually grilled against the mug, I start to do a little tap-dance of agony on the carpet. Sighing deeply, Eunice sits up further in bed, reshapes her triangular back-pain pillow, then picks up her hardback (*How I Lost 600 Pounds In Six Weeks On The Idaho Nine-Bean Diet* by Flatula Tailpipe) checks the page number, folds down the corner and places it gently on the bed beside her.

"Now, place the tea down there," she says.

I virtually drop the mug onto the table, and insert my scalded digits between my pyjama-clad thighs.

"Bernard, stop whimpering. If you had the gumption to bring up the tea on a tray like a normal person, you wouldn't have got burned, now would you? Go and run it under the tap."

So while I stumble into the en-suite to extinguish my smoking flesh the harangue continues. I really can't believe it. Never mind that I got up at 5.45am because the cat was scratching at the door, never mind that I actually am kind enough to make her tea and bring it to her, never mind that I'm bringing in the only money this benighted household ever sees, everything that goes wrong is my fault. She won't be happy until I'm dressed up like a room-service waiter with a linen napkin over my wrist, and a silver tea tray with a teapot and two china cups.

Finally I emerge.

"It's no good waving it around, Bernard. That won't make it better. Go and fetch a bag of frozen peas, and hold it in place for ten minutes. I've got some aloe vera you can put on it."

"Aloe vera? It sounds like a cockney greeting."

"Very droll. Now chop-chop. It's in the drawer downstairs"

"Which drawer?"

"The kitchen drawer."

"Which kitchen drawer? We have several." Indeed, since we had the kitchen expensively and extensively refitted by Möben we have more drawers than Madonna's boudoir. I am never able to locate anything. I start to wend my way downstairs and the braying voice follows me.

"Use your common sense, Bernard."

"I could be hours looking for the damn stuff. I have no idea where you keep it or what it looks like."

I open a drawer and riffle noisily and one-handed through knives and forks. "It's not here. I can't find it."

"Well it's hardly going to be in the cutlery drawer, is it?" is the shouted reply. "And don't bother with the drawer to its left, which is baking sheets, icing materials and pastry cutters."

"Are we going to go through this like some process of bloody elimination or are you going to actually tell me where this life-saving gunk actually is?"

"Don't you shout at me Bernard! There is no need to raise your voice. I'm trying to help!" she bellowed.

I find something called Nivea in a drawer by the sink. "Is it this Nivea stuff? It does say it is a skin cream."

"No. It's aloe vera. Oh for goodness sake." One minute's thunderous descent finds Eunice, dressed in housecoat and fluffy slippers, standing next to me as I open the seven-hundredth drawer full of knick-knacks and detritus.

"It's not bloody here," I say, sifting through mounds of cocktail sticks, drink swizzlers and decorative candleholders.

Eunice walks past me and opens the cupboard next to the fridge. "Here it is Bernard, you can stop panicking now."

"But that's a cupboard. You clearly said a drawer. A drawer slides, and that damn thing was hinged. I mean how was I supposed to find it? You've just sent a man with third degree burns on a wild goose chase."

"Do stop exaggerating. It was a hot mug. You make it sound like a napalm attack in the killing fields of Cambodia."

Eunice opened the top of the bottle seized my hand and splotted a great squirt onto my fingers. "There we are, is that better now?"

"It still bloody hurts, if that's what you mean. You fed me misinformation, which delayed my treatment."

"You'd better tell Social Services then," Eunice retorted. "If you're lucky they might take you into care and you could sit in Ebbing Tide Homes with the other geriatrics, waiting to be fed liquidised foods on a plastic spoon by underpaid and over-worked care staff. I'd not be unhappy to be shot of looking after you with your ridiculous demands."

So for the next hour we continued with the withering row, with me in my pyjamas with greasy fingers and a packet of frozen peas, and Eunice complaining about how unreasonable I am.

 Elevenses: Walked out to the local bakers and ate two fresh cream slices, with fondant custard, strawberry filling and a layer of icing. Felt much better.

Wednesday 20ᵗʰ February: Getting Up

Eunice is feeling particularly bleary-eyed this morning. Naturally, I am to blame. Over breakfast I feel her accusations crystallising while she sips coffee, and stares sullenly over the top of my *Daily Telegraph*.

"How many times did you get up to go the loo last night?" she asked.

"A couple of times I suppose. Why?"

"Bernard, it must have been more than that. You woke me at least three times. It's very inconsiderate."

"Well, if you hadn't left the ironing board in front of the linen basket I wouldn't have kicked it."

"Have you seen the doctor recently about your prostate?"

"Er. Yes, I think so. It's fine."

"When?" she said with sudden intensity. "You didn't mention it to me."

"It was December I think." This is of course a lie. With Eunice so involved in Christmas shopping I'm hopeful she won't have kept any record to disprove this. However, as Eunice's eavesdropping and surveillance skills would put the Stasi to shame, I'm not overly optimistic. Then of course there are the famed interrogation techniques, with which I was soon re-acquainted.

"What date in December?"

"I don't recall. It was a Tuesday, I think."

"Which doctor?"

"Actually, no. The NHS finally got its act together. They had a properly qualified one this time. No leopard skin headdresses or ju-ju charms, I'm relieved to say."

"Bernard. Which doctor did you see?"

"Dr Parkinson."

"On a Tuesday? He only works Wednesdays and Fridays. Are you sure?"

"It might have been Dr Rahman."

"For goodness sake Bernard. Which was it? Do you seriously expect me to believe you can't tell the difference between a six-foot Lancastrian cricket fanatic on the verge of retirement and a 30-year-old Bangladeshi woman who always wears a sari."

"Oh. It probably wasn't Dr Rahman then."

"No, I don't think it was. I don't think it was anyone at all. You haven't been to have it checked, have you? After all I said to you about it being the biggest killer of men."

"Marriage?"

"Prostate cancer!"

"I haven't got cancer."

But perhaps I am suffering from a terminal case of marriage. If only there was somewhere I could go to get a cure.

Thursday 28th February: Cave-In Cost

City Link, which last week said it would do no more re-deliveries for me, has contributed to an earnings collapse at Rentokil that was almost as spectacular as the 'great dining room cave in' of Endsleigh Gardens. I just wish I had been able to 'short' the shares because now I'd have had enough money to cover the cost of getting the builders to fix the ceiling.

Wednesday 5th March: The Buffett Way

All is misery at the share club as we contemplate an ever-falling market. Chantelle, working longer-than-ever hours behind the bar, breaks the news that she can't continue to make her monthly contributions to the club. Club treasurer K.P. Sharma shrugs, noting that Harry Staines has not contributed a penny for six months, while Martin gave up when his IVA began.

"So it's just you, me and Mike Delaney," I say. "I hope you've corrected for our increasing share of the assets."

"I have," K.P. says. "Of course this is crazy. We've got £1650 in cash in the account. If everyone had contributed as they should have done we'd have more than twice as much. With the FTSE at 5800 there are loads of bargains just waiting to be snapped up. Some banks are on incredibly juicy dividend yields."

"This from the man who got us to buy Northern Rock," murmurs Harry Staines, without looking up from *The Daily Sport*.

"No, I mean others like Royal Bank of Scotland."

"Ah, the next Northern Rock," Harry chuckles.

"Look," says K.P. "We should be optimistic about lower prices. We've got to behave like Warren Buffett."

"But I already do," says Martin Gale. "I've lived in the same house since 1958, I drive an 11-year old car and when I married Holly I bought her a ring from a discount catalogue."

"Did Buffett do that?" asks Chantelle. "What a cheapskate!"

"Yes, but Buffett owned the catalogue company, and a lot else besides," K.P said. "No, what I mean is that Buffett says he is more certain that buys are good value as prices fall. But if we don't keep our contributions up when the FTSE is low, we'll miss loads of bargains and just raise the average cost of the shares we buy. If we kept contributions the same, or better still increased them, we'd see the benefit of pound-cost averaging."

"Okay, I'll put a hundred in," says Harry, handing K.P. a roll of notes which he had prised from his back pocket. "But no banks, mind. Something safe, like a fag company."

"Safe for investors but not customers," I say.

"Whatever," Harry says. "That's Avril's housekeeping, mind. So let's not lose it eh, Rockefeller?"

Chapter Ten

Antichrist Antics

Saturday 8th March: Dot-To-Dot

This weekend is devoted to a family shindig, with my mother plus Brian, Janet and the Antichrist. Take them all out for a traditional afternoon tea in Tunbridge Wells. The place is modelled on a Lyons corner house, with waitresses in uniform and a Glenn Miller CD playing in the background. My mother is charmed, though can't stop herself asking whether the victoria sponge is made with powdered egg. She also asks for bread and dripping "as a special treat." The Antichrist, in a particularly vile mood, orders a slice of coffee and walnut gateaux, at the very 21st century price of £3.95, and then won't eat it because he claims he doesn't like coffee.

"Please eat it, Digby," says Brian, in his most emollient *Guardian*-reading tones. "Think of those in less-developed countries struggling to afford food because of biofuels."

"If you don't eat it, Digby, give it to your grandad. He loves cake," says Janet, trying to appeal to the malicious mite's competitive instinct.

Digby smiles wickedly and mashes the slice with his fork. "Here you are, Grandad. Nice and easy to eat."

"Ooh, you're a wicked one," says Dot. "That's a whole week's butter ration! You'd have been hung for that in the Blitz."

"It's alright Mum," I say, as I eat the still-delicious rubble. "Digby is going to pay for this, aren't you?" The child shakes his head, but he's wrong. I'm going to deduct it from my contributions to a stakeholder pension which I will be starting on his birthday. By the time he's 65, that slice of cake will have cost him £150.

Sunday 9th March: Digby Checkmated

As planned I take Digby over to see 'Perfect' Peter Edgington for a game of chess in the morning. We sit in Peter's giant conservatory, surrounded by pot plants while Geraldine serves tea, plus lemonade for the Antichrist.

"Urggh. There's bits in it!" says Digby, inspecting the glass.

"I made it with fresh lemons, dear," Geraldine says, miffed.

The game begins and Digby is immediately in trouble. His brows furrow and I see the telltale signs of a tantrum gathering as his ears go red. Peter is just poised to trap Digby's queen, when the child makes a sudden lunge and spills his lemonade over the board, sending pieces flying. However, he hasn't counted on Perfect Peter giant chess player's brain, which allows him to accurately recall the position once the board and table have been wiped. Digby lasts another five minutes and stamps off to the loo after being checkmated. He doesn't return for half an hour. "It's alright," Peter says. "I told him he could play games on my computer."

Oh no. That's surely the chess player's biggest ever blunder.

Monday 10th March: Bovis Satisfaction

Oh dear, oh dear. Bovis has missed forecasts. On the day of its results, I can happily watch them fall close to the 490p I sold them at in January. My son Brian remarked at the weekend that I now seemed to be agreeing with him about there being too many housing estates planned. Maybe it's my lost profits at Bovis, which I could have sold for 1200p had I seen the light, which are informing my opinions. Or perhaps it is my experience at the hands of the Harmsworth brothers, who cut down the precious pear tree on which I carved Amelia Wrigley's name all those years ago. That reminds me, I've read that they're going to planning appeal over the housing development at the Old Orchard. I think I'll write in to the council about that.

 Elevenses: As I eat a Club biscuit, I remember that I still haven't received that damn parcel from City Link. Looking at the last card I received I realise that I have to fetch it by tomorrow or they will return it to sender.

Tuesday 11ᵗʰ March: Pass The Parcel

Drive forty miles to a windswept industrial state and take half an hour to find the anonymous warehouse from which City Link plies its trade. I go into reception, which is as deserted as the Marie Celeste. After five minutes an acne-afflicted youth with earrings appears and I hand him the card. He disappears for a full twenty minutes. A wheezing woman then comes in and asks me if she can help. I tell her that someone is looking for my parcel, but hasn't been seen since 1903. She asks for the number of the parcel, which as I explain is only on the card. I describe the chav who took the card. She then pages 'Darren.' A bearded bloke in an overall comes in to tell her that Darren is on his break.

"But what about my book?" I say.

"I'll get it for you," says beardie. "Wossa number?"

"I don't know, Darren took the card," I say, with rising exasperation. "Can you just trace it from my address?"

There's a long pause, with sucking of teeth and shaking of heads. "You just can't do it without logging into the dispatch system," says the woman.

"Is that a problem?" I ask.

"It's down. Could you come back tomorrow?"

At this point, I'm afraid I blew up like Vesuvius. Finally, I returned to my car, and drove home like a demon. I got in to find the house deserted and a single delivery card on the mat from City Link: 'We called but you were out.'

Gaaaah!

Wednesday 12ᵗʰ March: Fed Up

Federal Reserve has pumped $436 billion of liquidity into the U.S. banking system to get them to start lending to each other. Loaning all this taxpayer's dosh to the nutcases who started the sub-prime disaster sounds daft. Won't they just fill their suitcases and head off to Las Vegas? It didn't even convince the stock markets for long, prices started falling again within 24 hours.

Thursday 13ᵗʰ March: Perfect Peter's Imperfect PC

Peter Edgington phoned me today in a state of uncharacteristic agitation.

"Bernard, I'm sorry to tell you this, but when your grandson came here on Sunday, I think he inadvertently changed some settings on my computer."

I knew this would happen. Peter had foolishly let the Antichrist, newly defeated in their chess game, play computer games on his PC while we chatted downstairs. I've had a nagging worry about it ever since. I'm quite sure that the one word that doesn't apply here is 'inadvertent.'

"What's happened?" I asked.

"Well, the default character set has become Cyrillic, the type size is four, the type colour is yellow and the background colour pink. It didn't take that long to undo it, but as soon as I rebooted the PC, it was back again! Then I discovered that all my website bookmarks were gone."

"I'm terribly sorry. He's not a very good loser, and he is rather clever with computers. I'm sorry to say it's unlikely to be an accident. He did exactly the same to mine, so I've now got it on password protection."

"But this is insufferable. Doesn't his father do anything about it?"

"Ah, Brian believes in letting the child's natural talents grow in an atmosphere untrammelled by creative limits. I'm afraid he's a schoolteacher of the *Guardian*-reading persuasion."

Peter harrumphs about this for a few moments, and then cheers up considerably. "Still, at least I slaughtered the little monster, didn't I? I shan't feel guilty about trapping his queen any more."

Friday 14th March: Profits With Dignity

Russell Traugh, the most irritating drinker at the Ring o'Bells, will no doubt be delighted that funeral director's Dignity, one of his share picks, has again produced excellent results. Profits shuffled forward by another 10%. The cost of death, it seems, is rising, just like the price of bread, eggs and milk. The company is now looking forward to the next decade when the national death rate is expected to rise as baby boomers start croaking in droves. I suppose this must be the ultimate contrarian play, but it gives me the shivers. Besides a P/E ratio of 21 and a measly 1.5% yield leave me colder than the Inverness Co-op's chapel of rest.

Monday 17th March: Misery Monday

The FTSE has fallen to just above 5400. Don't dare look at my portfolio, for fear of further depression. Plan to spend the rest of the day hiding in the loft, painting the water tank on the model railway layout and eating ginger nuts.

Tuesday 18th March: Disaster Hits Edgington

10.45pm Just about to go to bed when got a very alarming phone call from Peter Edgington.

"Bernard, I think I've been the victim of some kind of Internet fraud. Two of my bank accounts have been emptied."

"Oh how awful," I say, dying to ask how much he lost. Instead I ask: "What makes you think it is an Internet fraud?"

"Simply because the three smaller family bank or savings accounts which we don't use online are fine. It's only the ones which I use on the computer, including my main investment account. I'm extremely careful. I don't write passwords down, I never log in except on my home PC and I never fall for those phishing scams where they try to get you to re-enter security details on bogus sites. However, I've just got some new security software, and a scan on my PC detected a 'key logger'."

"Is that some kind of virus?" I asked, as a feeling of impending doom started to gather in my head. I just know the Antichrist had something to do with this.

"Apparently, they call it a trojan, which means once taken unwittingly inside the PC, it waits rather like the Greeks in the wooden horse at Troy. It watches you entering your account information and makes a copy of the keystrokes you use, which are then beamed over the Internet to some criminal mastermind who then logs in and empties the account."

"Good grief. It's absolutely staggering. Have you called the police?" I asked.

"Yes, after I called the bank. However, the reason I'm calling you is that scan showed the key logger was installed at 11.55am on Sunday 9th March. Which, as you know, was the day you brought Digby over…"

"Well, steady on, Peter," I said. "Now, I know Digby's a fairly naughty child, but this kind of thing is surely beyond him. He's not ten years old yet, I mean…"

"Bernard, I'm not saying he wrote the damn trojan software. But it does seem likely that while surfing online he may have come across one of those dangerous websites and unwittingly downloaded something. The fact that he deleted the browser's Internet history and my bookmarks is somewhat incriminating."

"I'm shocked, I really am…"

"My main worry, Bernard, is that banks normally reimburse those who are victims of online fraud through no fault of their own. But letting someone else, non-family, use the PC unsupervised could be construed as like leaving the window open for a burglar. Given the amount of money at stake, I'm terrified that I'll not get a penny. I have to tell you that Geraldine is furious beyond all reason, and is rather blaming you."

As soon as I put the phone down, Eunice, in dressing gown and towel-turban started giving me the third degree.

"You didn't leave Digby unsupervised, did you?"

"No, of course not."

"You can't plead ignorance with me. You know he's a computer

115

whizz," Eunice declared knowledgably, before returning to the urgent nightly task of filing down her bunions.

"I didn't know where he was! I was in the loo when Peter gave him permission to play on the PC."

"Oh, Bernard, you know what a devious little imp…"

"Look. It's all very well you being a hindsight scientist. What's done is done. We can't do anything about it now."

"But Peter might have lost thousands. It's no good just sitting there like a sack of potatoes. You've got to do something!"

"What would you suggest? A single-handed jihad against the East European mafia? A Herod-like culling of all youthful computer geniuses? Or perhaps writing Peter a cheque for £424.17, which is all the cash in our current account, as some kind of loose change in compensation?"

Chapter Eleven

Special Excursion

Wednesday 19th March: Last Minute Offer

The share club was just getting into an in-depth discussion on what to do about our shares in Debt Free Direct, now known as Fairpoint, when we heard the characteristic whistling noise that marks the approach of Russell Traugh in his shiny acrylic Asda jogging trousers.

"Afternoon, losers," he said with a grin. "What black hole are you pouring money into today?"

There is a general chorus of 'shut up' from around the table, with an added 'bugger off' from behind the bar, where an overworked Chantelle is attempting to listen to the discussion while serving up pensioners' portion lunches of lasagne for a group of ramblers in the front bar.

"Listen, I've got a proposition for you lot," said Russell. "A very cheap city break in an historic coastal European city, lovely architecture, throbbing nightlife. Best of all, the beer only costs 30p a pint and a meal for two costs a fiver."

"Thirty pence a pint?" exclaimed Martin Gale. "Are you having me on?"

"And they have real ale as well as lagers," Russell added, enjoying the hold he now has on his audience. "Dark beers, a real brewing tradition for hundreds of years. What's more, I can get you flights for a penny each way if you decide today."

"Bound to be a catch," shouted Chantelle as she walked past with plates piled high with what looked and smelled like scorched linoleum. "You know what he's like."

"That's right," said Martin. "Knowing you it will be a weekend on a caravan site in Skegness."

"And the nightlife will be listening to the rap music pounded out by the drug dealers' BMW in the car park," added Harry.

"Well, what a bunch of old miseries," Russell said. "I've a good mind not to let you come. I could easily have filled up all the rooms with me mates from snooker, but no, I thought to myself, I'm sure the Ring o'Bells share club would love to get hold of this opportunity as they are so keen on bargains."

"So you are going yourself?" I asked, with mixed feelings.

"Of course I am. It's four nights away, rooms from five quid a night. All you've got to cover are food and drink, which like I say is dead cheap, and bits and pieces of taxes."

"Come on, let us in on the secret," said Mike Delaney, brushing cigarette ash off his care-worn grey cardigan. "Where is it?"

"Alright, it's Riga. Going tomorrow night, back on Monday morning. It'll be a laugh, I tell yer."

"Where the fuck's Riga?" asked Harry.

"It's the capital of Latvia," I said.

"Latvia?" said Harry. "Isn't that Colonel Gadaffi's place?"

"You're thinking of Liberia," said Martin. "Latvia's one of those little places in South Africa, I think."

K.P. Sharma had watched this exchange with growing incredulity. "You really are the most ignorant bunch I've ever come across. Thank God we're not doing much emerging market investment. Latvia is one of the Baltic republics, formerly Soviet territory. It's sandwiched between Estonia to the north and Lithuania to the south. Harry, Colonel Gadaffi is from Libya, in north Africa. Martin, Liberia is in *west* Africa!"

"And the place in South Africa you're thinking of, Martin, is called Lesotho," chips in Chantelle, pulling a pint of Guinness.

"Lucky I'm here to arrange it for yers," Russell said. "Couldn't trust you lot to find your way to a wet weekend in Penge. So who is adventurous enough to join me in a trip to this cheap beer paradise?"

No one spoke for a while. The realisation was dawning that the only adventurous part of the trip would be spending time with Russell, rather than being in another country, however obscure.

"I've heard good reports about Latvia," said K.P. "Many people speak English, and Riga is supposedly a pleasant and cosmopolitan city. There isn't much crime."

"So are you up for it then?" Russell asked

"Er, no. I have family commitments," K.P. said.

"Well, I'm game," said Harry.

"If it's really that cheap, so am I," Martin said. "It's the only holiday I'll be able to afford, that's for sure."

"What about you, Chantelle?" Harry asked.

"If you think I'd go on holiday with you, you've got another think coming," Chantelle said. "Especially having heard what you lot got up to in last year's club outing."

Memories of last year's round-Britain-romp in Harry's knackered Jaguar, with a giant saliva-drenched dog, remained seared into the minds of all concerned.

Russell, having assured us that the all-in cost is likely to be less than £100 a head manages to rope in Mike Delaney too. When it comes to me, I'm in favour but know I'll have to get Eunice's permission first.

"Look, Russell," I said. "I'll have to pretend it's about shares and investment or Eunice won't let me go. Can we say that we are going to look around some emerging markets companies or something? Otherwise she'll either ban me or more likely want to come too."

There is a collective groan at the thought of Eunice joining the party. Her 40-minute harangue of the members of the Ring o'Bells share club after a stripper was organised for my birthday last year will not soon be forgotten.

Wednesday 19ᵗʰ March: Evening Excuses

6.30pm. Eunice has prepared a particularly revolting dinner tonight. It looks like imaginatively arranged road kill, but is apparently grilled snoek on a bed of sautéed beetroot and endives with pistachio nuts. I take my first fishy mouthful and gag immediately.

"Don't be like that, Bernard. There's a whole week's omega 4 and selenium in that dish."

"It's somewhat bitter," I manage, not wanting to upset my spouse just before asking the favour of a foreign trip.

"It's from Irmgard's *Men's Health* cookbook."

"Ah, well that would explain it," I respond, taking a sip of the accompanying drink, which tastes like diluted stoat plasma but is apparently cranberry juice and soya milk.

"You see, Bernard, I'm taking care of your prostate and lower intestinal tract as well as your cholesterol. Really, you should be thanking me for putting right all the damage you do with those illicit cakes, biscuits and sweets which I know you still hide in and around the den."

"Well, thank you," I say. After eating as much of the food as I can stomach I bring up the subject of the trip.

"Darling," I begin gently, which of course immediately raises her suspicions. "An opportunity has come up through the share club to take a weekend away as part of our research into emerging markets investment themes."

"Not anything like last year's I hope," Eunice responds.

"Well, no, this one's abroad, in Latvia. A city break with hotel included, all for about £100 a head. That's a bargain, really."

"Oh, that sounds quite good. I think we should go. I've never been to any of the Baltic republics."

"Um, well. I'm not sure you'd like it, there's going to be some investment presentations, talks with businessmen, that kind of thing. You'd probably be bored. And it's ever so cold, minus something, bound to be. Do you know the sea often freezes along that part of the Baltic until April?" All this spills out rather hurriedly.

"Bernard. If your share club hasn't got any money, as you are always telling me, why on earth will local businessmen be queuing up to talk to you? And which of you speaks Latvian?"

"Oh. I think they mostly speak English. I don't know all the details, Russell's arranging it."

"But he isn't even in the share club, is he?" Eunice says. "This just doesn't make any sense. I just think you're trying to put me off. I mean we've not been abroad for months, and now you don't even want me to come with you when we have the chance."

"I'd love you to come, really. But it is rather short notice."

"Why, when are you going?"

"Tomorrow, and coming back on Monday."

"But Bernard, this weekend is Irmgard and Nil's party!"

"Oh," I fib. "I thought that was next weekend."

"Bernard, don't be so ridiculous. I wrote it in your diary months ago. You know full-well they are launching an online dietary advice service, and you know that I agreed ages ago that we would help them set up and run the launch party."

"Oh dear, that is tiresome," I say. "But you see I've already paid for the flights." This is also a lie, but I'm in too far now to back out. "I promised Russell that I'd help with the checking in, as there's quite a few of us going."

"But I've bought a new dress!" Eunice wails.

"Well you can still wear it, can't you?" I say emolliently.

"Don't patronise me, you old goat. Don't think I don't know what you're up to. Don't blame me if I end up being seduced by any of the sexy younger men that are bound to be there."

"Oh, have they invited North Kent Blind and Partially Sighted again?" I ask. I was only just in time to duck as the remainder of my dinner came hurtling towards me.

Later that night, I take the precaution of secreting my passport, wallet and a selection of clothes in a suitcase under my model railway in the loft. I wouldn't put it past Eunice to hide vital necessities to stop me going.

Thursday 20th March: Stansted Stand-Up

Stansted check-in is a miserable place at the best of times, but at quarter to eleven in the evening, it is truly depressing. Having shared a car, Harry, Martin, Mike Delaney and I arrive to find the queue for the check-in already substantial. There is no sign of Russell at all.

"Hi guys!" We look up to see Chantelle approaching. She's

wearing a skin-tight Spandex top and sporting spiky orange and purple hair. With her is a taller and rather shapely woman of perhaps 25, in high-heeled ankle boots and jeans, with an alarming Mohican cut of green hair and a racoon stripe of black eye make-up. "This is Stef," says Chantelle. "She's coming too."

"After what you said I didn't expect you to come," I say. "Why the change of mind?"

"Well, it's alright if you can bring a friend ain't it? I just didn't want to be the only woman, especially with the danger of getting cornered by randy Harry here. Stef's a red belt Tae Kwon Do, so watch out. Especially after she's had a few vodkas!"

"Where has Russell got to, Harry?" I ask, interrupting Harry from open-mouthed leering over Stef.

"Oh, I think he got himself a fast check-in without baggage. He asked if I'd take his bags through as mine, while he went ahead to get a place in the boarding queue."

"Hang on a minute," I say. "Ryanair charges extra for bags, doesn't it?"

Harry scrutinises the sheaf of papers with the booking reference that Russell has given him. "The evil bastard," he mutters, "The tight, scheming, evil bastard."

When we finally get to the Ryanair desk we discover that we have only had the most basic costs have been covered. We already knew that the 1p tickets were inflated by £15 of taxes. But we hadn't realised we were booked in as having no luggage, so are having to pay £12 a bag each way per person to get them through, plus an extra £3 per person desk fee. By the time Harry gets through with three bags, one for himself and two for Russell, he's livid.

"I'm already down more than the £100 quoted for the whole weekend, and we haven't left bloody Stansted yet."

We thought security would be a doddle at this time of day. Unfortunately, Chantelle and Stef are ahead of us, having to strip off boots and jackets and goodness knows-what piercings to be able to avoid setting off the gateway alarm. Finally, they are each searched by female security officers, while the rest of us wait. Visible underneath Stef's suede jacket is, according to Harry, "a very comely pair of jugs."

Eventually we get through into the departure lounge, and here we find Russell Traugh sitting at a bar, looking unusually smart in white shirt and jacket, and halfway down a pint of Kronenbourg. Harry marches up to him, 6'2" of anger, his face as livid as a strawberry. A ten-minute argument ensues, which ends in a compromise. Russell says he'll cover Harry's hotel bill to make up for the cost of the bags, and on the way back he'll pay for his own luggage. "Now," says Russell. "I think I owe you all a drink."

Such an offer, utterly out of character, disarms us all. "Surprised you'd pay these prices for beer," Martin said. "Thought you'd wait until we get to Riga where it's cheaper."

"Ah well, there's a method in my madness." Russell straightens his jacket and puts his old Costain photo ID badge round his neck. He then walks up to a large group of moustachioed businessmen at the other side of the bar, some with Polish newspapers, who have just bought a large round of drinks.

"Excuse me gentlemen. Anyone here flying to Poland?" he says, leaning over the table.

They nod, and Russell asks for boarding passes, and reads back to them the flight number printed on each. He nods and then tells them that the indicator boards are no longer working and due to a security alert they should go straight through to the gate. One man starts to drain his drink, but Russell says they should please go straight away because flights may leave early. The businessmen rush off, gesticulating at the boards and each other in frustration. Once they have gone around the corner, Russell calls us over to the table.

"I can't believe you," says Chantelle.

Russell sniffs each drink in turn. "Harry, Martin, untouched pints of Carling. Ladies, two double vodkas, one with orange, just a sip missing. Mike, no real ale I'm afraid. How about most of a pint of lager shandy?"

"I'm not drinking that," Mike says. "There's slobber on the glass. It's disgusting."

"Your loss," says Russell, draining it in one. "Besides, all of you, knock 'em back quick. We've got about ten minutes before them Poles come back looking for me."

"Christ, I thought Harry was a chancer," says Chantelle. "We've reached new depths today. Still, Riga here we come!" With that she and Stef knocked back their ill-gotten vodkas.

Friday 21st March: Rigorous Riga

Blearily I opened one eye. A wave of pain swam forward from the back of my head. A grey half-light filtered through thin curtains, accompanied by the distant drone of traffic. My watch, still on UK time, said 7.17am. Nearby I could hear breathing. Raising my head slightly, I scanned my surroundings. My attention was immediately hijacked by two brassieres lying on the bedroom floor. One large, white and very lacy, the other small with yellow flowers. There were other items of clothing scattered around, including a black high-heel boot, crumpled on its side, and a Spandex jacket. There was also something else, which after considering every other possibility, I decided really was a leopard skin thong. Despite the hangover, I felt a frisson of excitement, not for the moment recalling how I came to be in such an interesting position. I turned over, and reached out a hand with some trepidation. All I felt was a wall. Ah, yes. A single bed.

Last night seems a bit of a blur, but gradually it started to come back to me. I recall landing at Riga airport in the small hours, and all seven of us piling into a minibus. The driver had trouble finding the hotel Russell had booked. Chantelle and Stef had already bought themselves a bottle of vodka from God-knows-where, and were drinking it with a straw. It was passed around, and I took my turn. Only Mike and I had been prepared to pay Ryanair for a sandwich (salmonella and cucumber), so everyone else had been drinking on an empty stomach. The hotel when we eventually found it was a darkened doss-house behind the city's food market.

"This no good hotel," said the driver, peering at the cracked sign and grimy windows.

"No, it's alright," Russell said, starting to get out.

"No, not good. Very bad people here, make rob of you. You get proper hotel. You nice tourist, like nice hotel."

"Oi, Russell, have you booked us into a dump," yelled Harry. Eventually, much to Russell's protestation, we persuaded the driver to take us the two-minute drive to a decent hotel. The trouble was it worked out about £35 per room, and they had only two family rooms, each of which slept three, and a single, for the seven of us. Tightwad Russell wanted to find somewhere cheaper but the rest of us, dog tired, would have none of it.

"That's all right," said Harry, quick as a flash. "I'm happy to chaperone the girls and sleep on the couch."

"I don't *think* so," said Chantelle. "Nice try Harry. But that would be like putting Dawn French in charge of a Mars Bar warehouse." She and Stef had a quick whispered discussion and then chose me. "Bernard's the only one of you we can really trust to be a gentlemen. Well, sorry Mike, you are okay but you smoke."

Harry then demanded the single room, which Russell would have to pay for, while Martin Gale, Russell and Mike Delaney ended up sharing the other family room. Harry soon discovered the hotel bar, but only he, Martin and the two women had the energy for more drinking. Eventually, though I was persuaded on the grounds that I might as well drink with them, because if I turned in now I would only be disturbed when they came back drunk, as they were determined to be. So the evening had gradually dissolved away.

Someone in the room yawned and stretched. I turned my head gradually, and heard a body emerging from the bed near the window. A dark shape detached itself from the shadows, and gently slid the curtains a foot apart. There in the dazzling gap was briefly displayed a naked silhouette of womanly perfection. I drank in the smooth round bottom, breasts like inverted bells and the neat dark triangle at the top of Stef's rangy thighs. After a luxurious stretch, she turned from the window to scan the floor, lifting various items of clothing. I forced my eyes almost shut. Within a foot of my bed, so close that I could detect her delicious sleepy scent, she bent down and picked up a towel, which she quickly wrapped around herself. My heart was hammering, and a raging and undeniable lust was drawn towards the centre of my body. Stef padded to the mirror, ran quick hands through dishevelled hair, and then on into the bathroom. While Chantelle snored blissfully on, my head swam with erotic thoughts about her friend. A few minutes later Stef emerged wearing a bathrobe, drew back the curtains, and I felt able to offer her a feigned sleepy greeting.

"Got a bit of a thick head this morning," she said, grimacing. "How about you?"

"Slight headache and a bit stiff, otherwise okay," I replied, struggling to sit up in bed. "I'm ready for some breakfast though."

"I think we might have missed it," Stef said.

"I don't think so. It's only half seven in Britain and Latvia's two hours ahead, so it's 5.30am now."

"No, if Latvia's two hours ahead that's 9.30am. There's a bit too much daylight out there for 5.30am isn't there?" Stef said, displaying the kind of mental agility that today was well beyond me.

"Hmm. I think breakfast finished at 9am."

"So let's go out and get some."

While I took my turn in the bathroom, Stef got to work repairing her Mohican hair. By the time I'd emerged she'd stiffened it with gel to form a crest from her forehead right down to the nape of her neck. While I slipped on my blazer and brogues, Stef applied a touch of mauve eye shadow, grabbed her suede jacket and whispered goodbye to the still-sleeping Chantelle.

We emerged from the hotel into the genial warmth of a spring day. A church bell tolled in the distance as we set off into the cobbled streets of the old town. These medieval causeways were enclosed by gabled, heavy-roofed buildings but at the far end beckoned an open square, bisected by a tramline. There, near a large Orthodox church we found a bakery, and bought some extremely cheap blackcurrant tarts which we ate while sitting on a bench. We got quite a few stares from the locals. I suppose it's not everyday they see a crusty old duffer and a green-haired gothic beauty sharing breakfast.

"So tell me about this share club," Stef says. "Do you make much money?"

"No. I can't say we do. We sit around and argue about what to do. Half the time we act rapidly and decisively, and it turns out to be completely wrong. The other half the time we're too late to do the right thing. It's a bit frustrating actually."

"Right."

"So do you invest yourself, Stef?"

"No. Haven't got the cash. What I do have is just in the building society. I think the stock market's a bit of a casino."

"That would explain why we've lost most of our chips then," I responded glumly.

Friday 21st March: Off Your Trolley

11am. Back at the hotel another argument is brewing, this time about beer. Harry is fuming at the cost of drinks, and it is Russell once again who is in the firing line.

"You said that the beer was 30p a pint, you lying toe-rag," Harry said. "I paid 2.8 lats for a half litre last night. That's nigh on three quid."

"I know, I know. I was just going on what the guidebook said," Russell replied. "Prices have obviously gone up a bit."

"A bit!" Martin exclaimed. "At that rate I'm only going to be able to drink a tenth of what I planned."

"It'll be cheaper away from the touristy bars," Russell said, perusing his well-thumbed copy of the *Rough Guide to Latvia*.

"Let's have a gander," said Chantelle, prising it from his hands. "Is this all you've got?" she said. "It's bloody ancient. Published in 1996! No wonder the prices are out of date." As she held up the book, a great sheaf of pages slid out.

Russell grabbed for them, but Stef was quicker. As she scooped them up she found some other papers that had dropped out. "Well, well. Look what I've found." She showed around a flyer that had been concealed in the book. It had a woman on the front, naked except for a strategically placed Latvian flag, knotted into a pair of knickers. Russell made a grab for the flyer, but Stef quickly passed it behind her back to Chantelle.

"You dirty bugger, Russell," Chantelle said. "Listen to this everybody. 'Riga stag experience. Lovely ladies to your liking. Sauna and strip, sensuous, no-holds-barred massage...'"

"Oh my God," she tittered. "They've even got topless paintballing! And someone's written a little asterisk against it!"

Russell again grabbed for the flyer, but Chantelle handed it back to Stef who raised it high over her head. With her 4 inch heels it was beyond Russell's reach.

"Come on, gissit 'ere." muttered Russell.

"Now I begin to get the idea of why you've all come here," Chantelle said. "Were all you perverts in on this?"

"Well I wasn't," I added, truthfully.

Mike Delaney shook his head.

"First I've heard of it," said Harry, trying to look innocent.

"But it was you who told me," said Martin.

Harry looked heavenward. "For God's sake! Why can't you keep your mouth shut for once?"

"There's nowt wrong with having a bit of fun," Russell said. "We work hard and we play hard. It's as simple as that."

"You don't work hard," said Martin. "You skive off when no-one's looking, and sometimes when they are."

"What about your budget?" asked Stef. "This'll cost you more than you expect if you're still working off 1996 prices. Strippers don't come cheap."

"Oh, I don't know," said Harry. "There was a girl I knew in Naples in 1961 who'd let you feel her up for a Woodbine. For a full packet she'd take off her wooden leg and show you..."

"That's quite enough, Harry," I said. "Ladies present."

"Where?" said Harry, scanning the hotel lounge. "I thought it was just us."

Stef giggled. "You really push it right to the limit, don't you?"

"Well I don't know about you, but I've got plans," said Mike Delaney, waving a much more modern Lonely Planet guide around. "Anyone fancy coming with me to the Museum of the Occupation?" Mike described the 50 years that Latvia was controlled by foreign powers. From 1941 to 1945 it was the Nazis, and from then until 1991 the Russians. Chantelle and Stef opted to go with him, while Russell had other plans.

"That's too depressing for me," he says. "There's a motor museum. That should be a laugh. What d'yer reckon Harry?"

"I've heard there is an ethnographic museum," said Stef. "That would be right up you're street."

"What's ethnographic? Is that like ethnic pornography?" Harry asked, then whispered to me: "I like girls of every colour, even green," he said, inclining his head towards Stef.

"Well, ethnography can be stark, confrontational and explicit," Stef said. "It's a raw and naked look at who we are and where we came from. I did it as part of my degree."

"She's a bit of a girly swot," said Chantelle.

"Well," said Harry, rubbing his hands with glee. "I'm up for a bit of raw and naked looking."

Russell gave him a thumbs up, and they both looked quizzically at me. I nodded in agreement. I just wanted to be there to savour their disappointment.

Friday 21st March: Jab At The Hut

4pm. Back at the hotel, both Harry and Russell are feeling hoodwinked. We'd taken a tram and two trolleybuses in order to get to the ethnographic museum, and twice ended up in the wrong place. By the time we had found the museum, in a wooded area by a large lake, it was clear that ethnography wasn't quite what Harry and Russell imagined.

"It's just a collection of wooden shacks," said Harry. "I don't believe we've come all this way to see that load of old cobblers."

"You must admit it's quite pleasant though, seeing all the different types of wooden houses that make up the country's architectural heritage," I said.

"You were in on this, weren't you Bernie?" Russell said. "You knew what ethno was, dincha?"

"I knew it was about culture and society, so you were likely to be disappointed. I'm afraid she's made a monkey out of you both."

Saturday 22nd March: Disco Queen

Recollections are hazy. Four bars, a Russian restaurant, more bars. Lots of dark beer, then whisky, then vodka. Good grief. I recall being in a disco. I don't know how we got there. Most of us were comatose at a table. Martin Gale was unconscious, slumped forward with his head sideways on the table. Mike Delaney had gone back to the hotel. Russell was wobbly, and had the still-wet stain of an entire bowl of beetroot soup down his best shirt and jacket. I don't recall how it happened, but it looked like he'd been shot, and had delayed us getting into the night club as the doormen tried to steer him to the nearest hospital. Only the two girls had any energy. Stef and Chantelle had been dancing with two drunken Russian businessmen for the last hour.

Stef was quite a sight. Tonight she'd avoided the gel and the heavy make-up and let her shoulder-length hair hang loose (of course, it was still bright green, and matched her high heels.) She was wearing a skimpy singlet and short skirt, which showed off her fabulous legs and sinuous curves as she gyrated to the pulsing sound. Chantelle, who'd been to school with her, said she was known as 'Stef the body', in the sixth form. I could see why. Chantelle, who must be the only person who ever pogoed to Gloria Gaynor's *I Will Survive*, was having more trouble keeping with the pace. However their partners, grey suits patched with sweat under the armpits, were the first to give up. The two Russians thinking their chances were good, followed the girls back to our table, and insisted on buying rounds of vodka. They introduced themselves as Yevgeny and Valeri.

"Valerie? That's a girl's name in England," said Harry.

"Nyet," said Valeri, the beefier of the two. "Not Val-urry. V'leery. Man's name. Means to be strong, healthy." He thumped his chest for emphasis.

"So you're on the pull, like?" said Russell.

"Pull?" said Yevgeny. "What is pull?"

"Is pill, Yevgeny," said Valeri. "He wants know you have pill."

"It's alright, darling," giggled Chantelle, putting her hand on Yevgeny's hairy forearm. "I promise you won't get pregnant."

Until this moment, I hadn't noticed either a) that Chantelle was even drunker than most of us, or b) that she seemed to like the hairy Russian, despite his moles. Fearful for Chantelle's honour, I intervened: "So, are you fine fellows married? Do you have kids?"

"Married, no," said Yevgeny, with a sly look at his colleague. "Kids, nyet. However, Yevgeny, he have Ket. Pussy ket, called Katerine." At this point he dissolved into sniggers.

"Not Ket. Is dog," said Yevgeny. "Is bitch."

"Don't listen to them lot," said Chantelle, pointing at us. "They're just trying to spoil my evening."

"No, we're trying to stop you spoiling *their* evening," laughed Harry. "When they find out what's underneath."

"Not that *you'll* ever find out what's underneath," Chantelle said, hands on hips. "You're just jealous of them."

"No, I'm not." said Harry.

Chantelle took her Russian beau onto the dance floor for a smoochie number, repeatedly sticking two fingers up to Harry behind her partner's back. Stef, meanwhile, wobbled off to the loo.

"Hey, Valerie," Harry said. "You're doing alright there."

"Beautiful green-hair girl," Valeri said, his bloodshot eyes going wistful. "I want make love from her."

"The only trouble is," Harry whispered. "She's got clap."

"Klep. What is this klep?"

"Disease," Harry said, pointing to his groin. "Down there."

The Russian's face contorted in disappointment. "This klep, is AIDS?"

"No, it's even worse. It'll gnaw your todger off in five minutes."

"Todger?"

"You know. Cockski, St Petersburglar,"

"Huh?"

"C'mon mate, y'know. The old turnip trumpet, the meaty Mig, the beetroot baton, the Smirnoff javelin."

Valeri looked utterly baffled.

"He means your virile member," I interjected, pointing at his trousers.

"Ah," he said. "My buj. Is bad for me?"

"But he's lying. It isn't true. He just being vile," I added.

"Now the other girl," said Harry. "She's actually a tryborg."

"You mean cyborg, Harry," I said. "Half human, half robot. Is that the joke?"

"No tryborg," Harry insisted. "Half human, half tram."

He whispered conspiratorially to Valeri. "Listen, you'd better let your mate know. There's more metal in Chantelle than in the Trans-Siberian railway. Her how's-your-father's made out of a tin-opener."

Despite my protestations, this wall of spiteful propaganda was taking its toll on Valeri's mood. When Yevgeny and Chantelle came back, breathless and arm-in-arm, Valeri pointed to his watch. There followed a brief but animated conversation in Russian, and he and Yevgeny stood up to go.

"Where are you two off to?" wailed Chantelle.

"Bye-bye, lovely Chantelle" Yevgeny said. "Late. Sleep now."

When Chantelle turned to Harry, I had never seen her so angry. "What have you been saying about us?"

"Nothing," Harry responded.

"Bernard, has he been horrible?" she asked.

One look at my face showed her the truth. Chantelle burst into tears and stormed off, cursing Harry for spoiling her holiday, and the only chance for romance she'd had in several years.

"Well done, Harry," I said. "Do you always have to be vile?"

"Well, what does she want with a Russian anyway. He'll only treat her like dirt. If the Russians can shaft a canny operator like BP, they can certainly do it to her."

"Yes, but I think she actually might have wanted it to happen," I said.

Saturday 22nd March: Two A.M.

By the time Stef returned from the toilet, Harry had already stalked off, Russell had disappeared, and I was left with a sleeping Martin Gale. Chantelle had apparently sobbed her heart out to Stef in the ladies, and gone home.

"So it's just you and me then?" Stef said.

"Well, and him," I said pointing to Martin's recumbent form. "Two's company, three's a debt-ridden corporation."

"Fancy a last dance?" she asked.

"I can't dance. Not to anything written after 1905 anyway."

"Anyone can dance," she said, pulling me to my feet. Almost immediately the music changed to a slow number, and I tentatively put my arms around her. With her heels, we were exactly the same height. Her piercing blue eyes were quite bewitching, while the slow rotation of her hips against mine and my drunken state gave me ideas, indeed sensations, that I really shouldn't have had.

"So were you upset that Valeri went off?" I asked.

"Not really," she said. "I was just making up the foursome for Chantelle's sake. "They were obviously married and desperate for a roll in the hay." She paused and gave me a direct look. "Not that I'm always averse to that."

Staggered by the magnitude of the possibilities just opening up for me, I stumbled onto Stef's foot. She tottered sideways, and I realised that the heel of one shoe had fractured.

"Oh, I'm dreadfully sorry," I said. "Here let me help you."

I brought her back to the table where she found a use for the broken shoe, tapping Martin Gale on the head. "Wakey-wakey. Time to go home."

Somehow all three of us staggered out and found a taxi. At the hotel, we dragged Martin up two flights of stairs to his room and plonked him on his bed, waking up both Russell and Mike Delaney in the process. One more flight and we were back outside our own room, within which Chantelle could be heard moving around. I fumbled for the key, but Stef stayed my hand.

"Not yet," she said.

In one quick movement, she pulled me close to her and sank her mouth onto mine. The kiss was so hot, wet and potent that I had to grasp the door jamb for support.

"I'm very, very drunk," Stef said. "But I do really like you. I've always liked older men. Even through this mist of vodka I can see that you are the one male on this trip that has behaved with complete decency."

"That's very nice of you to say," I replied.

"You know, I'm so drunk, that if Chantelle wasn't already in there, I would probably drag you in and rip all your clothes off. I think we can both agree, though, that it wouldn't be a good idea."

"Well, I'm not sure..." I said, desperately wondering how Chantelle could be removed from the room, by persuasion, force or teleportation. My thought was extinguished by another kiss, even more passionate than the last.

"I mean you are married," she whispered, between nibbling my neck. "And you've probably been very faithful...to your devoted wife...who I don't even know...and I don't really know you."

"Well, Stef, this really is a wonderful surprise." I said, watching her large breasts crushed against the front of my shirt.

"The other thing," she said, "is that in the morning I can blame all this on drink. But right now I think I have to rush to the bathroom because I think I'm going to be sick."

"Unfortunately," I said, opening the door, "that is the effect I have on most women. Even when they are sober."

Sunday 23rd March: The Morning After

Another grisly hangover, but the sweetest sensation as I pieced together the night's happenings from drink-addled memories. I took an al fresco breakfast alone, walking the streets of Riga on a warm and spring-like day. I didn't really see Stef until mid-morning when I returned to the hotel. She gave me a rather sheepish smile, and took me aside.

"I'm so sorry about my behaviour last night," she said. "I'm a bit wicked when I'm drunk. I do hope you're not shocked."

"I have no complaints. None at all. I will treasure the memory."

"Discreetly, I hope? That's very important."

"Absolutely. Mum's the word."

Sunday Afternoon: Taxing Conversations

I found the group sitting and chatting on the sun lounge of the hotel, looking as if they didn't have a care in the world. Chantelle was looking her usual bubbly self, and very much appreciated the bunch of pink and yellow roses from the market that I gave her to cheer her up.

"What a gentleman," she said.

"They were actually very cheap," I said, feeling a slight blush.

"It's the thought, ain't it?" she said, staring at Harry. "And not even an apology from the bloke who really caused the trouble."

Eventually, she did get a grudging apology from Harry, who seemed to be quite excited about something else.

"I ran into your Russian fellas again today, you know? Valerie and the hairy one. Did a bit of business."

"Oh yes?" said Chantelle. "Trying to find their secret to charming the other sex. Something you have never, ever had."

"Funnily enough, yes." Harry held out his hand across the table. In it was a handful of blue diamond-shaped pills.

"That looks like Viagra to me," said Martin Gale.

"Well it's not Bob Martin's is it, sonny boy," said Harry. "I'm going to buy some regular supplies. They're offering them at about a fiver for 20. In Britain, if you can get it at all, it's a fiver a pill."

"How do you know they're the real thing?" said Mike Delaney, taking a deep drag on a cigarette. "They could be forgeries."

"Well, I'm not stupid," Harry said, with a smile on his face. "I already planned for that..."

"No I am bloody well not available, and neither is Stef," Chantelle said. "Just in case that's what you're thinking."

"Relax, darling. I already tested one last night. Solo."

"So you were doing business last night?" Chantelle said.

"Of course. I latched onto that comment they made about the pill, which you thought was a contraceptive. When Yevgeny was at the bar, I talked to him about it, and he let me have a free sample."

"So now you've done the deal, what are you going to do?" Stef asked.

"Well, it's a nice little business isn't it? They'll post me the goods, I'll get a website set up, hosted out here but all in English. No tax problems, legit-sounding import-export. You know," he tapped the side of his nose.

Chantelle explained to Stef that Harry always had these amazing business ideas. "Tell her about the motorbikes," she said. So Harry proudly told the story about rushing down to Devon in January 2007 when a freighter ran aground, and salvaging a crate containing two undamaged BMW motorcycles which he sold for a fat profit. He then ran on with another anecdote about how he helped Martin Gale set up his Bulgarian wine re-labelling business in which empty Bordeaux bottles were stolen from the recycling bins of posh restaurants, refilled with cheap red, re-corked and sold for laying down for a minimum of ten years.

"That certainly helped bring in a few pounds to meet the debt repayments," Martin added. "And no stealth taxes on that lot."

Harry stretched his arms, re-set his sunglasses and adjusted his chair to soak up the last of the afternoon rays. "Yes, I really can't complain. My little sidelines have done pretty well, except the shares of course. They're a disaster."

"That's a pretty impressive income, Harry," Stef said.

"Yeah, well. Not bad," he said.

For some reason, Chantelle was absolutely beaming like she'd won the pools. "You know, Harry. I'm so glad you're not the shy, modest and retiring type. You love to talk about yourself, but you don't ask any questions. Do you have any idea what Stef does for a living?"

"I thought she said she was a public sector office worker."

"I am, in HM Revenue & Customs," she said. For a good minute everyone's jaws hung open.

Harry looked mortified. "I didn't know they had such quality crumpet working for 'em. Well, Stef, don't snitch to anyone senior will ya. We don't want the tax inspectors breathing down me neck, do we, eh?" he tapped the side of his nose.

"Harry, I *am* a tax inspector. In special investigations," Stef said. "I recovered £14 million of black market money last year, third highest in the country, from an undercover operation."

"Chantelle, you little cow. You did this deliberately, didn't you?" Harry said. "You set me up!"

"Look," laughed Stef. "I'm on holiday, right? I can't be doing with this now. It's not really my department. But, for the record, here's the deal. If you want to import Viagra into the U.K. do it through official channels. As for the other little businesses, when you get back, send a letter of full disclosure of all your undeclared earnings to your tax local office. If it's volunteered, they'll take a charitable view, probably."

Harry looked very sullen, arms folded.

"Cheer up Harry," Stef said. "We are human you know. Flesh and blood. And we do need a little love from time to time."

And at that moment she gave me a sly little wink.

Monday 24th March: Happy Landings

Back at Stansted, and sober for the first time in four days, we waited at the luggage carousel with mixed feelings. Russell was feeling down because Harry had forced him to pay up for luggage fees and the upgraded hotel, which meant he had no longer made a profit on the arrangements. Martin Gale was nursing a giant hangover and the unexplained loss of his wallet and his remaining £60 during the evening at the nightclub. Mike Delaney, loaded with cheap cigarettes, looked the happiest of us all. He'd even managed to both experience all the Latvian culture and remember it. Chantelle had finally forgiven Harry for his rumour mongering, and had to agree that in the cold light of day Yevgeny wasn't much of a catch. After her exposure as a tax inspector Stef had been treated as radioactive by Harry and Martin.

"That's why I don't tell anyone about what I do," she admitted to me. "Prejudice against tax staff is about the only one that is still rampant in our politically-correct world. I do a good job keeping our schools and hospitals funded, but you'd think I was stealing from people they way I get treated."

"Well, I'll never think of HM Revenue & Customs in the same way," I said. "If you ever feel like doing a detailed investigation into my affairs, I'm happy to comply."

Our goodbyes were interrupted by the sound of cursing. Harry Staines was wrestling from the carousel a broken, wet crate from which liquid and fragments of glass were falling. So much for the cheap vodka he'd hoped to be able to sell to friends and relatives. All in all, we'd spent far more money in Latvia than we thought, drank even more than we expected, but had more fun. As for me, I'll have to keep to myself the most special memory: the hot lips of a tax inspector.

Chapter Twelve

Grain Of Truth

Tuesday 25th March: Not Helping With Inquiries

Peter Edgington rang to say that the police weren't interested in following-up Digby's use of his computer, and the downloading of the virus 'key-logger' which emptied his bank account. The off-the-record advice from the local chief inspector was not to tell the bank that anyone outside the family had used the PC, even though it was with permission. Contacting the fraud squad, the officer said, was "a complete waste of time for this kind of crime." However, Peter admitted that he had already told his bank, and sure enough its policy is to reimburse only when the PC was used by a family member and, moreover, to insist that failing to supervise Digby would count as 'lack of reasonable care'.

 Elevenses: Eunice, back early from Waitrose, almost caught me in flagrante with a Cadbury's Flake Easter egg. However, she was so excited by the gossip she'd heard that she barely paid attention to my furtive swallowing. She had run into Daphne Hanson-Hart in the Fairtrade coffee aisle who had heard, via Geraldine, that Peter's bank account losses were over £48,000. Good grief! That is far more than I feared.

Wednesday 26th March: Share Club

Share prices are recovering, and the debate on what to buy is heating up. Chantelle wants more mineral companies, K.P. Sharma is after banks, while Martin Gale wants to buy commercial property. I suggest food and drink companies. Still, the share club has only £1750 and that includes Harry's £100, taken from his wife's housekeeping.

Thursday 27th March: Mother And Child

Dreadful day. Crawled round a rain-swept M25 to Isleworth to see my mother, who has summoned me for an expedition to the Morrison's hypermarket. I've got the blue badge on the dashboard, but all the disabled parking bays are occupied by tattooed youths in Vauxhall Astras, buying cigarettes and lager. Fuming, I park in the last mother and child bay, saving a five minute walk from the next available space. As I help Dot out of the car, a people carrier pulls up behind. Inside are about a dozen rioting children, mouths rimmed with melted chocolate, kicking, fighting and screaming. A fat and florid woman emerges, and she's furious.

"Oi! That space is for muvvers with kids," she bellows, over the ululation of her urchins.

"That's right. This IS my mother. I am her child."

"It's for mum's wiv toddlers," she says, waddling out of the vehicle. "And you're not a f***ing toddler. You're a f***ing adult."

"Good lady, my mother is a toddler. She toddles more slowly and with greater need than any of your jungle troupe of ill-disciplined gibbons and baboons, who I daresay could swing straight into the supermarket without touching the ground."

Without further ado the woman kicked me hard on the kneecap. "Now you can effing toddle," she muttered, as I crumpled to the ground in agony. She then calmly climbed back in her vehicle, casually walloped three of her offspring, and drove off.

Too shocked to respond, I staggered with Dot to the in-store café where a cup of tea and a danish pastry calmed me down. Fifteen minutes later, still limping badly, I was ready to tackle the supermarket. My assailant (easily tracked by the noise of her kids) was in the frozen food section, so Dot and I started elsewhere. While I kept an eye on my enemy, Dot seemed to be on a slow-motion trolley dash. Already aboard were ten two-pound bags of flour, five of sugar, three dozen eggs, 20 tins of condensed milk, four giant bags of toilet rolls and ten sliced white loaves.

"Mum, are you planning a surprise party for the Royal Anglian Regiment or something?"

"What's that Bernard?" she said, struggling with a catering-sized sack of basmati rice.

"Why are you buying all this food? You don't eat normally enough to keep a gnat on life-support."

"There's a famine, Bernard. The *Daily Express* says so. Flour, bread, everything. It's all going up in price, so I thought I get plenty in. I expect that we'll be back on ration books by Christmas."

"But rice, Mum? You've never eaten anything but tinned Ambrosia. Are you planning to open a curry house?"

"No. But by next week you won't be able to get it."

"But if you don't eat it, what's the point?"

"For swapping. I mean, look at Rhodesia, with money worth nothing. If I run out of something, I can swap my rice, or a toilet roll for a tin of chunks or some pilchards. Rice will keep its value better than my savings now, won't it?"

Suddenly I realised that my mother wasn't so daft after all. In her own make-do-and-mend way, she's preparing for a barter economy. That gives me an idea to finally get her to part with some of that inheritance.

Saturday 29th March: Biofuel Innovation

Arrive at my mother's house full of ideas of how I can prise some money out of her share portfolio and into mine. However, as soon as I've sat down with a cup of tea and a brace of chocolate Penguins, Dot hauls a heavy carrier bag out of the kitchen. Inside I see at least 20 tins of Morrison's own-brand sweetcorn.

"There you are, Bernard. It's part of your birthday present."

"Well, that's very kind," I say, thinking that she's having one of her more dotty days. "I'm actually not a huge sweetcorn fan, but Eunice is certainly very partial to her five-a-day."

"Oh, it's not actually to eat. It's for the car. I know petrol's very expensive, and you could save yourself some money by running the car on this."

"Volvo's can't cope with sweet corn, Mum. It has to be petrol. You know, from the filling station." Oh God, she's really gone doo-lally this time.

"Bernard, they run their cars on sweetcorn in America. It said so on the BBC," she said, as if that removed all possibility of debate. "All the farmers are growing it for fuel. It's all the rage."

"Mum, they use corn to make ethanol which is a kind of petrol additive. You can't just put it straight in, not like this."

"So it's cornflour then? Like gravy, except made with petrol?"

"Well, sort of." Giving up on my attempt to explain, I turn to the subject of investment. Dot has, as I realised in last week's shopping expedition, taken in the idea of a world food shortage. Her hoarding of flour and rice shows that this is a subject to which she is receptive. So I suggest that she should take £50,000 of her funds and instead set up a joint investment account with me which we can use to beat inflation by investing in commodities.

"But where would we store them, Bernard? The shed's almost full, and the cellar's loaded with old rubbish."

"No, Mum. What we'll do is to invest in funds which have positions in important food commodities. They will store them, but our shares will show what we own."

"I hope they'll be careful. Geoffrey bought a case of corned beef in the war from a spiv, but all the tins were bashed in. And dried egg, you've got to watch out for damp."

"I'll make sure they understand," I cooed, barely able to suppress my excitement that I'm pushing at an open door. "Now all you have to do is get Mary Asterby at the WI to help you sell..."

"I'm not going to sell my shares," Dot says. "Mary would be upset. She's been helping me, and she doesn't like you."

The feeling is mutual. I could strangle the interfering old bat for frustrating me when I'm so close. I rest my head in my hands while Dot heads off to the kitchen. There's some clattering, so I go in to see she has dragged out an ancient and dusty Bovril box from under the sink. Digging underneath a box of candles, a pair of blackout curtains and rolls of masking tape, she grabs an old Fox's biscuit tin labelled 'nuts and bolts'. I help her lift it out. It was very heavy, and must be crammed full of metallic bits and bobs.

"What's in here, Mum?"

"Oh, it's just a few old coins, pfennigs, drachmas and pesetas that Geoffrey accumulated. I brought it up from the cellar last week. I thought we could put the money into your ration fund."

"Well, most of it won't be legal tender. We'd be lucky to reach 50p, yet alone fifty grand." I prised the lid off. There were safety pins, tiepins, cuff links, plenty of ancient small change, including threepenny bits and even a ten bob note. However, most of the space was taken up by a cardboard box tied up with ribbon. Inside that were about 100 coins, each wrapped in tissue paper. I unwrapped one and gasped. It was golden, emblazoned with a maple leaf design on one side and the head of Queen Elizabeth on the other. Most important of all, it said 'fine gold one oz'. I unwrapped each in turn. I was speechless.

"That's old Canadian money isn't it?" Dot said. "Looks like chocolate money for the Christmas tree. Is it worth anything?"

"It certainly is! If they each contain an ounce of gold that's nearly $100,000 worth. Did you know about these?"

"Well, I know Geoffrey bought some gold around the time of the oil crisis, but I didn't know what he did with it. He complained that no sooner had he bought it, then it halved in value."

"Well, it's a perfect start for our commodity 'ration fund', that's for certain."

Monday 31st March: ~~Hornby~~ Warning

Supplier delays in Asia and a weakening of demand in the UK have hit my Hornby shares, knocking them well below 200p. Still, I'm so busy getting the application forms together for a joint stockbroking account with my mother that I could hardly care less. In the Hornby drawer there is a box of 100 gold coins, current sterling value around £47,000. Yippee!

Chapter Thirteen

Coining It!

Tuesday 1st April: April Fool's Gold

Today is my 65th birthday, and I'm finally rich. My deranged mother, having blocked my inheritance for years, has allowed me to take away 100 Canadian Maple Leaf gold coins that we discovered in a tin of otherwise worthless foreign coins. The proceeds will be invested, in line with her wishes, in commodities. She has in mind tins of Spam, Bovril, dried egg, Persil flakes and Be-Ro flour. I'm thinking palm oil futures, gold mining shares and Russell's Ukrainian stock pick, Landkom. I'm lugging this lot into town today to get them authenticated, and I'm so deliriously happy about it that at 7am, after letting in and feeding the cat, I return to bed and whispered to my still-dozing spouse that I was available, immediately and without pre-condition, for birthday hippopotamus manoeuvres. Eunice lifted her eye mask, looked suspiciously at the clock and sat up in bed to remove her curlers.

"Is there something in the tea, Bernard?" she asked.

"No, I'm just happy. The sun is shining, the birds are singing and the world is a marvellous place."

"Come on, whose pre-tax profits have come in well above expectations?"

"No idea. I've not even been on the PC yet."

"Has Gordon Brown resigned?"

"Not yet, I fear."

"I bet you've borrowed some of those funny blue tablets from Harry Staines, you naughty boy!" She snatched at my bathrobe and pulled the flaps apart. Her face fell. "Hmm. Nothing here that Vodafone would want to mount a transmitter on."

"Ah, but all third generation equipment," I responded.

Still, after a shorter than usual delay the matrimonial act was briskly consummated. Casualties were light: a twinge in my lower back and a jolt of sciatica in Eunice's left hip. As so often these days, the tea was still warm by the end.

Elevenses: Arrived at the bullion dealers at little after 10am. Greeted and shown into a room where a woman confirmed what I already suspected from my Internet searches, that these were original Royal Canadian Mint solid gold coins. The buy price was £457, that's lower than the selling price of £479 quoted on the website, but never mind. This is a gift horse whose dental condition I have no intention of inspecting. Celebrated with a Thornton's dark chocolate Easter egg, half price, which I devoured in its entirety on the train journey home, as a gaggle of jealous schoolboys looked on.

Monday 7th April: Vengeance On Rentokil

With thousands now cleared into the bank, I've decided to go on a shopping spree. First stop, a short-spread bet on 1000 Rentokil shares at 95p. Eunice's blasted book, which I ordered for her birthday in January, still hasn't arrived. I presume that City Link has lost it or sent it back to the publisher. After getting nowhere with customer service (surely the most oxymoronic of corporate terms), it seems the best way of getting even is to devalue the parent company's shares. This is the first use of my spread-betting account since the disastrous Marks & Spencer short-selling fiasco, but there must surely be some other over-priced candidates where hope exceeds reality. It's just a question of finding them. I am interrupted in my musings as Eunice comes in holding a copy of *The Independent*.

"Hamsters doth cringe," she says, enigmatically.

"I'm not surprised, if that's the publication shredded on the floor of their cage," I respond.

"Five and seven. Something, something, Q, something, something," she says, squinting at the paper.

"Is this one of the paper's characteristically offbeat lead stories, or are you trying to solve some puzzle or other?"

"Cryptic crossword, Bernard. Irmgard's done most of the clues, and lent it to me to finish."

"Look, you know I can't do cryptic puzzles," I say, turning back to the PC screen.

"What do you mean? Your entire life has been one long cryptic puzzle, devoid of meaningful clues for those of us around you." And with this general insult hanging in the air, she stalks out.

Tuesday 8th April: Spending Spree

Have turned my eyes completely square doing a top-down analysis of commodities. Have decided that oil is the most reliably in short supply, so buy 1000 shares in BP at 535p and 1000 in BG Group at 1280p. For metals, I choose 500 BHP Billiton, which is racing ahead at £16.66. I also decide that leading food companies must be able to force price increases through, so bought 1000 Unilever shares at £17.10. That will allow me to tell Dot that we've cornered the market in Marmite, Bovril and Persil ready for the return to world war two rationing she has long predicted.

Wednesday 9th April: Members Only

Arrive at share club full of high spirits after investing my mother's commodity cash, and offer to fund a round for all members. However, the crackle of cheap trousers moving fast reveals that first at the bar is none other than Russell Traugh. The Ring o'Bells' own resident Yorkshireman is cheekily demanding a treble Courvoisier. However, Chantelle is serving and she's no fool.

"That's £6.90 please, Russell," she says brightly.

"Cobblers! Bernie's buying this round. I heard him say so."

"Russell: Club-Members-Only," she said, enunciating each word through her black-lined lips. "You've never joined."

"C'mon, pet, I'm as good as in. Look at all the share tips and free advice I've offered you lot," Russell said.

"Unwanted advice, insultingly dispensed," noted Martin.

"You bunch of wazzocks. I should be treated as an honorary member, for God's sake," Russell whined.

"C'mon. £6.90, quick," Chantelle said. "People are waiting."

"Well, I'll have a lime and soda instead then," he grumbled, fishing out a grubby 20p piece from his pocket.

Chantelle put the brandy glass behind the bar, and poured the lime and soda. "So, that's £7.90 altogether."

"But I'm not having the brandy now!" Russell squeaked.

"I've already poured it. It won't go back in the optic, will it? Cough up now, or you're barred!"

"And a bluddy pound for a lime and soda, what a rip-off," Russell groaned. We all watched as he fished in a back pocket, and pulled out the most mangy banknote we had ever seen.

"Sorry. Don't take Scottish," Chantelle said. "House rules."

"It's legal tender, you gothic horror story!"

Chantelle responded by taking a good swig from the brandy. "Cheers, Russ. Another insult, and I'll finish it."

Grumbling continuously, Russell pulled out an ancient wallet, held together with packing tape, and connected by a long chain to his Traughmatic Abrasives jacket. None of us had ever seen it before, and indeed were not likely to see it again. He took his one and a half drinks and stalked off into the front bar.

K.P. Sharma meanwhile is urging us to look at banks. "They're discounting every piece of bad news," he says. "Look at Royal Bank of Scotland. £3.70p each, yielding 8.9%! Come on Bernard, now that you've got your winnings, how about contributing a bit more into the club? It'd be very contrarian."

Harry says: "K.P. can I just say two words?"

"I know, Northern Rock," sighs K.P. "But there has to come a bottom, and you can't recognise it until you're past. All you have to go on are fundamentals. There really is an awful lot of damage already in the price."

I tell them that I'd still prefer a candidate to go 'short' on. I mention my foray into Rentokil, and ask for other candidates.

"What about Punch Taverns?" says Mike Delaney. "This place has been quieter than a grave since the New Year. Maybe their other pubs are down too."

"Yeah," says Chantelle. "I know what the problem is. Too many Russells, not enough Bernards."

Saturday 19th April: Antichrist Refuge

We're off to see Brian and Janet for the day. Eunice nagged me throughout the entire journey about my 'lack of appreciation'.

"You haven't worn that lovely cravat that I bought you for your birthday, not once in two and a half weeks."

"Well, I'd just feel like a refugee from *The Amorous Prawn* expected to say 'Rath-er' every two seconds. Besides, crimson's not really my colour."

"Bernard, you have no idea. Your wardrobe is drabber than a Volgograd council estate. A splash of colour would do you good."

She joined sartorially critical forces with Janet as soon as we arrived, and while Brian was on vegetable peeling duty I took refuge with the Antichrist in his bedroom. With the PC now removed, as a just penalty for his damage to Perfect Peter's bank accounts, Digby has renewed an interest in tabletop war gaming. However, looking more closely at his figurines it seems they are a mixture of science fiction and Dungeons & Dragons, using mythical beasts armed with flamethrowers and first world war tanks.

"It's called Warhammer 4000," he says. "You could take me down to Games Workshop and I could show you how to play, if you like. I could let you have some of my Smarties too, Grandad."

The mendacious mite certainly knows my weak points. No doubt I'll be expected to buy him something from Games Workshop too, but it certainly beats discussing my wardrobe with my own dragon, so I'm game. Besides, it'll give me an insight into this odd retail phenomenon which has in the past proved quite profitable for investors in the company.

Chapter Fourteen

Monsters From Hell

Sunday 20th April: A Kick In The Warlocks

Took my grandson to Games Workshop for a war gaming day. Saw an astonishing collection of devils, imps and goblins, and that was just the children. The good-natured staff, treated as free child-minders, seemed happy to lead the tabletop mayhem in which intricately painted miniatures did battle amid convincing scenery. Digby's army, largely made up of evil rat-men known as skaven, was outnumbered by the ogres and beastmen of a skinny bespectacled ten-year-old called Trevor. Still, the Antichrist did well until he was ambushed by dark elves, whereupon his warlocks took an almighty bashing. Digby yelled repeatedly in frustration while tiny Trevor tutted at him.

"You should grow up," he said, stroking his chief troll. "Learn to lose gracefully."

Digby's reddening ears alerted me to impending violence and I was able to scoop him away before he swept everything from the table. Having delivered the Antichrist home, I looked up Games Workshop shares and saw they have been recovering reasonably well from weakness earlier in the year when the dividend was cut. Though the products look as enticing as ever, it isn't as compelling a cost-cutting story as others. *Chronic Investor* says 'High enough' which is hard to argue with.

Monday 21st April: Keeping Abreast Of Rivals

Eunice is spring-cleaning the den. That means mayhem for all my papers, and probably a dysfunctional PC afterwards too, after the vigorous scrubbing she is giving screen and keyboard. I'm about to visit the downstairs loo, but discover that she's stacked two boxes of annual reports and Prescott, the giant stuffed pig, on the floor.

Hearing my protestations, Eunice comes in to see me trying to manhandle Prescott out of the door.

"Bernard, please leave Prescott there. He's got bulimia and he needs the loo more than you do."

Eventually I return to my desk and after rebooting the PC discover two profit warnings. One, I'm delighted to say, is Rentokil, the stock on which I have had a short position since 7 April. Yet, on checking the share price chart, would you believe it, the shares rose from 90p at the open to 97p? How can a dismal company like this warn of a 'significant full year loss' instead of a break-even and be rewarded with a higher price? I absolutely do not understand the stock market sometimes, I really don't.

I take some comfort from the other profit warning though.

This is Sport Media Group, the firm that Harry Staines last year boasted was growing profits by 250% a year and had a P/E ratio of eight. But the shares, down 11½p to 30p today, and are a long way from the 76p that Harry bought his at, and the culprit seems to be too much competition in the world of adult content. Hmm, I wonder. Just as I'm clicking on the paper's website, the doorbell goes.

"Would you get that, dear? I'm tied up at the moment," I say, as a graphic image of a young woman in stockings fills the screen.

The only reply is the suck and roar of the vacuum cleaner upstairs. Finally I trudge out to the front door to see a card being pushed through the letterbox, and the familiar but elusive yellow and green of a City Link van sitting outside. Exploding into action, I fling open the door and tear after the driver in a blur of paisley slippers. He stops just before getting into the van, and I finally take delivery of Eunice's book, *A Gentlewife's Guide To Pleasing Her Spouse*, by Lady Lucinder Mockett, which I had ordered for Valentine's Day.

Elevenses: Two raspberry and cream tarts from the independent baker in town, in commiseration of the fact that I got the right share to short, but the market got it wrong.

Tuesday 22nd April: Rights And Wrongs

Royal Bank of Scotland has launched the rumoured £12 billion rights issue that just a few months ago we were told wasn't ever going to happen. I don't really know what Tier 1 capital is, but I'm just glad that we didn't listen to K.P. Sharma at the share club. If we'd bought the shares as he recommended then we'd not only have lost a wodge of cash in the falling price, but would have needed to stump up extra lolly for the rights just to retain our share of the bank's profit. It's all very well talking about 11-for-18 at 200p, but what does it actually mean to shareholders, and how can we work out whether it's value for money? I would normally ask Perfect Peter Edgington this kind of question, but after the Antichrist's devastation of his PC, I suspect that I'll be *persona non grata* for a long time to come. Perhaps K.P. himself will be able to walk us through the calculations, because you don't see it in any of the papers.

Wednesday 23rd April: Deutsche Bonk

Hell's Bells share club this week is devoted to K.P. Sharma showing us how to work out rights issues. As he says, companies don't explain what such things as ex-rights prices mean, nor make explicit that dilution usually means a dividend cut.

"The RBS announcement doesn't say that it's going to cut the dividend," says Martin Gale, looking through a hefty printout. "It just says they will pay out 45% of earnings in dividends, about the same as 2007, which was 33p."

"Ah," says K.P. "But those same earnings will be spread over a lot more shares. So if you got 33p in 2007 and there's an 11/18 rights issue, what are you likely to get per share in future, assuming the overall earnings are stable?"

Martin, sucking a pencil, looks stumped and scratches his head. Chantelle, today resplendent in pink eye shadow to match her hair and a new lip piercing, is the one who's on the ball. "It's 33p, times 18 divided by 11 plus 18, ain't it?"

"Yes, but you express it most easily by summing the denominator, so 33 x (18/29). The answer is 20.5p," K.P. says.

I struggle with the maths, but it's clear that even with the average price of the shares being lower because of the rights issue, dividend dilution is going to cut the yield to 7%.

"Now K.P., I remember that you wanted us to buy RBS," notes Chantelle, as she munches through some scampi fries. "But if we did, we'd have lost money on the share price fall, have to stump up more cash for extra shares, and get lower dividends. All for a bank with poorer growth prospects than we were led to believe after the over-priced takeover of ABN-Amro."

"You summed that up lovely, darling," says Harry Staines. "Here's another reason not to buy banks," he says, stabbing a finger at the crumpled *Financial Times* on which he's been resting his pint of Adnam's. "It seems Deutsche Bank will no longer reimburse the cost of brothel visits for staff'," he chuckled.

"Good grief," I say. "So what was the old policy?"

"Just imagine," he said. "You know what Germans are like for recording details: a separate expense claim code for every sexual position, and maybe a Hamburg-weighting allowance. If travelling abroad you'd have to share your totty with a colleague unless you were entertaining clients, and do the currency translation yourself.

You'd have to work out the VAT so they could claim it back, and those bods in Health & Safety would want not only receipts for the condoms but a written declaration that they'd been used, to avoid HIV impairment charges on the bank's human assets."

Friday 25th April: Looking After Nasdaq

Jem has dropped in to tell us that she and Toby are off on holiday to Mikonos. Oh yes, and would we be kind enough to look after Nasdaq for them for two weeks? This is a typical example of my daughter's thoughtlessness. Their black labrador, as energetic as his stock index namesake, is only six months old and needs vast amounts of exercise. They have only left enough of his dry food for two days, so that's another subsidy I'm making.

Saturday 26th April: Ga-Ga Over Grangemouth

Got a phone call from my mother, terrified that Britain was going to run out of fuel because of the impending strike by refinery workers at Grangemouth. Found it very hard to shut her up.

"Really, Mum, what are you worried about? You don't have a car and you've already hoarded enough food to supply a nuclear bunker full of Sumo wrestlers."

"But what about Maurice?" she says. "I depend on him."

"Maurice runs on batteries, not petrol. Don't you remember I showed you how to recharge him?"

Frankly, I'd be happier if my mother got rid of her mobility vehicle altogether. She's a liability to herself and to all road and pavement users. Only last week I was walking with her along the Great West Road when she veered off the pavement to inspect what she thought was a packet of smoked salmon lying in the bus lane.

My shouts that it was in fact a flattened pigeon fell on deaf ears, and might have been on dead ones had I not leapt into the carriageway to wave my arms like a lunatic to warn traffic.

Close of play: The new Jones family commodity fund investments are going rather well. BHP continues to climb, at 1800p from the 1666p purchase, Unilever is essentially flat, but BP is the real star, having climbed to 580p ahead of next week's results, giving me a 10% profit already – about £500. Now that is really something to celebrate. So now I have decided we shall call the fund DotCom, from my mother's name as chief funder, and from commodities, which is the mast we have nailed our investment flag to.

Tuesday 29th April: Best Estimates

Narrowly escaped a hippopotamus manoeuvre this morning. Pinched a well-honed tactic from the enemy: feigning a headache. Of course, with Eunice this meant having to needlessly subject myself to a detailed cross-examination, down several Nurofen, lie with an ice-cold cloth on my forehead and rub some revolting camomile and horseradish gunge (that Irmgard recommended) into my neck. Only after I'd won an Oscar for my 40 minutes of unrelenting moaning was I signed off marital duties.

While Eunice was in the loo, I escaped downstairs at 8.10am, grabbed a coffee and logged on to the PC to see what the world of shares had to offer. Astounded to see that BP has beaten all forecasts with a 44% rise in profits, with $6.6 billion in the year's first three months compared with the $5.2 billion that analysts were expecting. Stayed to watch the shares, constantly refreshing the price page and urging the chart ever higher. I have to admit this financial voyeurism gave me more ecstasy than anything that happens to me while pinioned underneath my wife. Does this make me odd? Not if you've seen her, it doesn't.

My reverie was interrupted by Eunice bursting into the den, in bathrobe and towel-turban. I immediately threw my hands to my head. "Ow, ow, ow. Why doesn't it stop?" I crooned. "It's like a rusty nail from one ear to the other."

"Bernard, you obviously can't expect to throw off the pain if you're looking at a computer screen. They're notorious for eye-strain. Come back to bed. I've got some feverfew and milk-thistle lotion which should help. And no caffeine."

She and I both grabbed for the coffee, and in the collision that followed it tipped over the keyboard. There was a hiss and crackle and the screen went blank.

"Oh well, solved two headache problems at once," she said.

Wednesday 30th April: A Company By Any Other Name

After weeks of debate, the share club has finally decided that it is today going to spend its accumulated fund of £2837.14, come what may. However it is only when K.P. Sharma gives us each a print out of where we stand that we notice what has happened to some of our previous investments.

"Blimey," says Chantelle. "BT's down by a third from when we bought. Have people stopped making phone calls?"

"And what about this Fairpoint. When did we buy that?" asked Martin Gale. "What happened to Debt Free Direct?"

"You lot never listen do you," K.P. said. "I told you before that Debt Free Direct changed its name."

"But look at the price!" Martin squealed. "It's only a quid and we bought it at three. Am I the only person with an IVA to support this industry?"

Chapter Fifteen

Car Alarm

Thursday 1st May: Goodwill Over-Paid

Hornby has just bought Corgi, maker of die-cast models. Ah! I well remember my 1950s collection of milk float, Scammell low-loader and Bentley, with which I used to manufacture level crossing disasters during the days when I still called my layout a train set. I really can't see what today's PlayStation and X-Box generation would want with them, but as Hornby says it is really a collectibles market, for nostalgic old buffers like me. However, before going too misty-eyed, I'm amazed that for £7.5 million Hornby is getting only £1.4 million of assets. Trademarks, intellectual property, goodwill and so on do have a value, but there's a limit to what you can do with them when a collectibles market depends on scarcity. I'd never have fallen for that one. When I bought Four-eyes Filton's pram-dragster in 1955 for one-and-six, I didn't fall for that nonsense. He wanted an extra thruppence because it had an early version of ABS brakes (powered by his sister's knicker-elastic) but I wasn't having any of it until I had the chance for due diligence, which involved being pushed down Tall Hill on it. Pulled bleeding out of the nettles at the bottom, and minus one molar, I declared that I was keeping my thruppenny bit.

Elevenses: Tentatively bit into an ancient Netto fig roll, one of many hidden in the layout's big tunnel upstairs, during the biscuit wars. In recent months they have been used on my goods trains, one per truck, to simulate a cargo of concrete. Indeed, having bitten into it, that is what it has become. I return the item to its truck, and go downstairs in search of softer fare.

Saturday 3rd May: Renault Lost

Elevenses: Quietly munching away on a bar of Toblerone while Eunice is out. I thought I'd be safe for several hours as she has gone on a single-handed Barclaycard-funded mission to drag

Britain's retail sector out of recession. Now that she knows I have money from Dot, she's lost all sense of restraint. However, the phone rings and it's a breathless Eunice on the line.

"Bernard, the car's been stolen! I left it in the multi-storey and when I came back with my first few purchases from M&S, House of Fraser and Debenhams, it was gone."

I'm almost as alarmed about the idea of successive waves of purchases too big to be carried about as I am about the loss of the car. Further questioning reveals that she's certain that she's got the right floor, despite not making a note of it, because it was between a silver Golf and the fire exit, and now there's a blue Mondeo in her spot.

"So, would you be good enough to come and pick me up, Bernard? I've got more bags than I can carry."

"Please just check the other floors. Just to be sure."

"Bernard, there are seven floors in this car park, plus the half ones on the other side, and I parked the other end from the lift."

"But I'm not going to drive all the way there if it turns out your Clio is just a floor away from where you are."

"Well it's really come to something in our marriage if you don't trust me anymore. The car's been stolen, I'm lost and alone in a strange place..."

"You're in Bromley for Christ's sake, not Faluja."

"But I saw a hoodie outside Next. Anything could happen to me and you just don't care." The telltale signs of snivelling began, so I finally relented. And guess what? When I got there she was in the wrong bloody car park. The Clio was just where she left it. But whose fault was it? Of course, you guessed. Mine.

Wednesday 7ᵗʰ May: Medical Appointment

Just about to head off for share club at the Ring o'Bells, when Jem arrives. She breezes past me with barely a hello, and gets into an earnest and apparently medical conversation with Eunice. I return to the den, somewhat baffled, and only emerge when the sound of car doors banging indicates further activity. Finally, when Eunice is just getting into Jem's car I wander up to ask what's going on.

"I'm taking Mum to hospital," says Jem.

"Can I help with directions? You go round the M25. Then take the A30, turn off just after Camberley heading for Crowthorne, Broadmoor is just off the A3095."

"Bernard," says Eunice, testily. "I've told you goodness knows how many times, I've got my screening appointment today."

"A screening?"

"About my lump. Look, Bernard, do I have to shout it down the street just because you never remember anything?"

"A mammogram!" hissed Jem.

"You're wasting your time Jemima," Eunice said. "Bernard probably thinks a mammogram is a new Post Office service to keep him in touch with his mother."

Thursday 8ᵗʰ May: Unileverage

Unilever, a major part of the DotCom fund, has reported a 35% rise in earnings per share, and has taken action to recover the cost of commodities. As hoped, this company has the leverage to hold its own against the supermarkets. BP, Billiton and BG Group, the other elements in the fund, also seem to be doing well, so at last I have a workable investment strategy.

 Close of play: Made about £430 today. That's the ticket!

Saturday 10ᵗʰ May: Antichrist Cluster

Family get-together, arranged by Jem to be supportive to Eunice, who as I'm repeatedly told is going through a 'difficult time' with medical worry. My sister Yvonne's come all the way down from Stockport, while Brian and Janet have ferried over the Antichrist to keep us all on our toes. I've done my bit, buying Eunice a big box of Thornton's best, making pots of tea and patting her on the back on numerous occasions. Digby, having asked to use the den this morning, emerges with a hand-painted egg box filled with hand-made Belgian chocolates. He basks in the praise for some truly out-of-character behaviour as we devour the lot. However, when we get to *my* chocolates, the box ribbons are curiously awry, and the cellophane gone. All seems well until we delve into the second layer. Instead of lemon parfait, coconut paradise and chocolate dream there are just empty spaces.

"What a swizz!" I say. "They've only given me half a box."

"Oh, I should take it back," says Yvonne, eating the last almond marzipan from the top layer. "Trade descriptions, isn't it?"

Eunice chuckles: "While my nine-year-old grandson is able to get me hand-made Belgian chocolates I can't trust my husband to get me a whole box of shop-bought."

Some cog in my brain clicks, and I look at Digby, who is looking particularly smug. Why, the cunning little...

Tuesday 13ᵗʰ May: Energy Savings

For the fourth time in a fortnight, I am going to have to drive halfway around the M25 to see my mother. She's phoned up, having got into a state about the energy efficient bulbs she was given by the council. She can't seem to fit them.

"Can't you just use the existing ones for now?" I ask.

"No. The council man said it was very important. Apparently the police can tell who's been using too much energy through their carbon fingerprints."

"Carbon footprints, Mum, not fingerprints."

"Anyway, Mrs Harrison and the Dentons at number 37 have got their bulbs, and keep them on all day just so we'll notice. Well, I don't want to look bad, so I'm washing me nets and I'll have mine on display too."

So, cursing the price of petrol and Gordon Brown's eco-drive with alternate breaths, I drive round to fix things for her. My carbon footprint for this journey alone probably amounts to five years'-worth of savings from her energy efficient bulbs, but I can't begin to explain that to her. When I do get there I see she's been supplied with screw-in bulbs when she actually needs a bayonet fitting.

"Didn't they give you any bayonets?" I ask.

"No. I think they gave them all to the Home Guard."

It takes me another ten minutes to straighten that one out, and another fifteen minutes on the phone to the council to explain that Dot needs the other fitting. On the journey home I notice that the price of petrol at the roundabout has gone up 3p since I last passed it just an hour ago. Unbelievable! The way things are going I'll only be able to afford to do this journey in Maurice, Dot's mobility vehicle.

Wednesday 14th May: The Final Purchase

Warm weather at the share club, so we sit outside at the Ring o'Bells, allowing Harry to use his 'totty screener' to assess the merits of the women walking by.

"That's an Ashtead," he says, peering at a forty-something bottle-blonde. "Used to have attractions, now expanded a bit too rapidly and vulnerable to a slowdown in spending. Cheap, though."

He then points out a large, worn-out looking woman besieged by her numerous children. "Definitely a BT. Top heavy costs, looks sluggish next to rivals, but resilient in tough times."

Harry then sees a mini-skirted brunette on a bicycle: "Now there's a BHP Billiton. Superb natural assets, buoyed by the commodity super-cycle, but mucky if we're lucky…"

At which point Harry's face is pushed firmly into his lasagne. Chantelle, holding it there, pours half a pint of dregs from the tables she's been clearing onto the back of his head. "Harry, your attitude to women makes the Taliban seem like Germaine Greer. Now if you were a share it would be JJB Sports – sagging sales, trouble in the fitness sector and distinctly unattractive."

Harry emerges with egg, and much else, on his face as the rest of us dissolve in giggles.

K.P. Sharma, calling the meeting to order finally insists that we must make a decision over whether to spend our small surplus or keep it for still lower prices. Mike Delaney, Harry, Chantelle and K.P. expect the market to fall further. I see it flat but wobbly, while Martin Gale, ever optimistic, thinks FTSE's heading for 7000. With most of us bearish, we decide to keep our powder dry. Perhaps the end of September will be the right time to commit the cash, after the summer doldrums are over.

Monday 19th May: Going For A Wii

Just as I suspected, the long arm of the American legal system has finally snagged BAE Systems' collar. Chief executive Mike Turner was detained by Justice Department officials at Houston Airport. Things called subpoenas were involved. Like gubernatorial, valedictorian and sophomore, such words are destined to mystify the English. Still, it's all about Al Yamamah, that's for sure. Though Dot wouldn't allow me to sell her BAE shares, I'm really glad that Mary Asterby of the Womens' Institute persuaded her to do it. This isn't over yet for BAE, mark my words.

Anyway, speaking of criminal investigations, it is Digby's tenth birthday today. The malevolent mite has been wheedling me for weeks, demanding to have 'a wee.' This was not a request for a visit to the loo as I'd first thought, but some piece of highly expensive computer kit. What Wii does, I cannot tell you, but apparently there have been lots of them sold. If it keeps him out of mischief, so much the better.

Tuesday 20th May: Planning For The Future

Apart from getting the Antichrist a 'Wii' for his birthday, I've made good on my plan to start him up a stakeholder pension. I'll be paying in £1 a week, on which I'll get tax relief, and he won't be able to lay hands on it for at least 50 years. Using the ready-reckoner spreadsheet that Peter gave me, and assuming 7.5% a year returns, the first year's contribution alone will be worth £6300 by 2058. Hopefully by then he will be less like a scheming third-world despot and more like a civilised human being. If not, there'll probably be enough money in his pot for him to buy a tropical island tax haven from which he can pillage the world through Internet viruses. By then I'll be long gone, but all I can vainly hope is he appreciates his old grandad who laboured long and hard under the MoD yoke to earn his own pension, only to see it frittered away by his wife, daughter and Gordon Brown. Perhaps if they've invented time machines by then, Digby can bring me some of the cash back!

Elevenses: In maudlin mood, I eat two lemon-iced cupcakes, a taste redolent of youth. Proust would have approved.

Thursday 22nd May: Question And Answer

Brian rings me to tell me the latest crisis in Britain's education system. I've long thought that GCSEs were handed out free with petrol or as consolation prizes on scratch cards, because there is no other way to explain why a nation of ignorant knife-wielding hoodies can get ever-higher marks. Now however, we hear the truth, as demonstrated by the GCSE music paper, that the answers are printed on the back of the exam papers.

Considering my own modest success in the General Certificate of Education, as it was then, I feel I can hold up my head proudly among today's over-qualified media studies 'yoof' who can't knot a tie, can't polish a pair of shoes, can't distinguish the circumstances when to use 'yours sincerely' and 'yours faithfully' nor manage a 'please' and 'thank you'. I can't see it will be long before pandering to the young will allow the first A-level in texting to enter the national curriculum.

Saturday 24th May: Ethics Girl

While looking up some investment funds on Trustnet, I stumbled across M&S Ethical. This is the fund into which, despite my protestations, Eunice plonked the remaining £4500 from her mini-cash ISA in March last year. Well, over that time the fund has fallen by 14.6%. That serves her right, quite frankly. Of course, if she'd invested it my own portfolio, I'd have lost her rather more. But they would have been good honest losses, not trendy ecological idealistic losses. At least I'm aiming to make money first, last and in between. Ethical funds have other priorities. I had assumed that the fund must have missed out on the minerals boom, because there's nothing these *Guardian*-reading types hate so much as mines in pristine rain forests, particularly when half the executives are either mates of George W. Bush or unrepentant white South Africans. However, I see that one of the largest holdings in the fund is RioTinto, which I'm sure I recall as being the most pilloried and hated of all the miners. Have things really changed so much that RioTinto has become winsomely ethical, or do we just have a new set of ethics? I remain baffled.

Elevenses: I'm just about to reach for my last cup cake in the Hornby drawer, when Eunice walks into Lemon Curdistan, completely uninvited. I quickly slam the drawer shut, and turn to face the invader who is armed with a J-cloth and Mr Sheen.

"Do you have a visa, Madam? Cleaning services aren't expected until Monday."

"Don't be tiresome, Bernard. I've got to dust today. I've got an appointment at the hospital on Monday."

"But I'm busy, can't you see?"

"Surely losing more of our money can be postponed until this afternoon. While I'm busy here, trying to keep this household from dissolving in filth, you could make yourself useful by putting away those clothes you left all over the bed."

"Can't you just give me a few minutes?"

My plea was cut off as Eunice stacked all my papers into a heap, dropped them on the floor and squirted her spray everywhere. Under such determined chemical attack, the forces of Lemon Curdistan were forced to regroup.

"As for losing money," I sniped from the safety of the hall. "You perhaps want to see what Marks & Spencer's ethical funds have done for you. I think you'll find that you've lost enough to buy a dozen pairs of St Michael elasticated trousers, twenty flowery blouses and a pile of underwear the size of the Great Pyramid of Cheops."

Chapter Sixteen

Hug A Hoodie

Monday 26th May: Tradesmen's Entrance

Oh thank you, Lord! An estate agent's board has appeared in the front garden of the O'Riordans, our troublesome neighbours. The moment I see it I feel like falling on my knees and prostrating myself to every known deity for this stroke of good fortune. I may not be a great fan of estate agents, but I wish them God's speed on this one. They will certainly be earning their commission. When I think of the O'Riordan's noisy parties, always rounded off at 5am with a 500 decibel karaoke rendition of *Una Paloma Blanca*, the behaviour of their horde of ginger children, and their abuse of that lovely au pair Astrid, I can't wait for them to go. Certainly, that bloody trampoline alone, with the vile screeching language of the catapulted occupants right next to our hedge, must have knocked more off the value of our home than the entire sub-prime mortgage crisis.

I recall one Saturday night at about 3am hearing a commotion in the garden, *our* garden. Armed only with a rolled-up copy of *The Spectator* I chased out several hooded youths from behind the shed. There I discovered the recumbent and barely conscious form of Bethany O'Riordan, surrounded by a half dozen empty bottles of Diamond White Cider. Still only sixteen, but like her friends she was clearly capable of supporting the drink sales of Matthew Clarke, and indeed its parent company Constellation Brands, throughout any recession. If only its other customers could be so resolute. Once I'd awoken her, and she'd been violently ill all over my courgette patch, it became clear from her dishevelled clothing that she'd taken David Cameron's advice about what to do with hoodies to a rather literal and extreme conclusion.

Now that it's clear we are losing our neighbours from hell I rush off to tell Eunice the good news.

"Yes, yes, Ken's run off with another woman. Didn't you know?" Eunice responds, flicking through the *Radio Times*.

"No, how was I supposed to know?"

"Come on, Bernard, keep up. Ken's car hasn't been there for months, has it? Lisa's going out with Shaft King Exhaust Replacements now.

"Pardon?"

"Shaft King. You see the van there all the time. He's the dark fellow with the hairy chest. Much better than the Kev's Carpet Tiles and Underlay, I reckon, though Daphne disagrees. She doesn't mind bald ones, so long as they don't have tattoos above the shoulders. The best though was that hunky young fellow from Rigby's Rod'n'Drain, but he only stayed for one weekend.

"I can't begin to understand how you know all this. Do you hide all day behind the azalea with binoculars, like Bill Oddie?"

"It's the only excitement I get, Bernard. Vicarious thrills are better than none. Besides, I'm quite restrained. Daphne says that from the skylight over her linen cupboard you can see Lisa's water bed. Apparently it's rough seas, most nights."

I immediately steer away from that subject. Still, the most baffling part of all this is why Lisa O'Riordan thinks Yellow Pages is a dating agency. No VAT of course, cash-only. The biggest question is who pays whom.

Tuesday 27ᵗʰ May: Market Knowledge

I walk into Lemon Curdistan after my morning constitutional to find Eunice at my computer, squinting over the top of her reading glasses at estate agents' websites.

"Excuse me, can I ask what you're doing?"

"Obviously, Bernard, I've been finding out what the O'Riordan's house is going for," she replied.

"Are you planning to buy it? Or are you just being nosey?"

Eunice turned around on the chair and stared at me. "It isn't nosey, Bernard, to establish the value of assets adjacent to your own. It's sensible. It adds to market knowledge, I thought you would understand that as an investor."

"And what have you discovered?"

"Five seven five. How much did they pay?"

"£425,000, I think. Two years ago."

"Well, they'll never get that, will they?" Eunice declared. "That would mean chez nous must be worth £600,000, because our conservatory's hardwood, not nasty cheap UPVC."

The amazing thing about all this is the sheer confidence of value embodied in Eunice's views. This from a woman who was gulled into paying £185 by a market trader in Oporto for a Louis Vuitton handbag which not only turned out to be fake, but whose handles dropped off after she'd loaded it with her cosmetics, curling tongs, eyelash benders, loose change and what-not. As I said at the time, it's just a shame that you can't buy an Eddie Stobart handbag. It may not have the cachet, but at least it can handle the load.

Thursday 29th May: The Plastic Fantastic

Daphne Hanson-Hart, the wheelie bin witch of Endsleigh Gardens, has now finally found something to take her mind of the state of council refuse disposal. She's come over for coffee with Eunice and they've been gabbling away about little else but the goings on at the O'Riordan house. I can hear them yakking away quite clearly in the kitchen, even from the den.

"Did you see the other morning?" Daphne said. "I was putting the blasted recycling bin out at 7.30, and there was a young man just emerging from Lisa's front door. He didn't look a day over seventeen. I mean, does she have no limits at all?"

"It wasn't the paper boy, was it?" Eunice replied. "You know that Bethany's been going through them like a dose of salts, don't you? She invited four of them in to watch Ken's old pornography collection when Lisa was out. That Joshua, you know he's only thirteen, looks a bit like Harry Potter. Well, his mother went round to complain to Lisa in high dudgeon, brandishing these DVDs which Bethany had let him borrow."

"Really?"

"Oh yes. She showed me them: *Surrey Sluts II: Confessions of a Woking Girl* and *Nymphomaniac Vampires of Chislehurst.*"

"Good grief. That sounds a bit worse than *Confessions of a Window Cleaner,*" giggled Daphne.

"Well it's all so artless, isn't it? One could get quite, you know, energised by seeing some bronzed and beautifully-filmed Italian couple making frenzied love in the dappled half-light of a Tuscan dawn on the sanded floorboards of their tastefully-furnished mediaeval villa, as the bells of the Capella di San Giorgio toll solemnly in the background. By contrast, the mechanical pool-side copulations and mock orgasms of plasticised Californians rather leave me cold. It's about as affectionately delivered as American foreign policy."

Daphne's guffawing now turned into a fit of uncontrollable honking, like some incontinent goose. When she'd finally recovered, she whispered: "So, what about Bernard, then Eunice? How does he perform on the sanded floorboards?"

"Nul points, as they say in Eurovision. I'm afraid to say that Bernard is terrified of sex. He'd rather scuttle away into the loft to play with his train set or hunch over some tedious share price screen on the damn computer."

"Oh dear. Have you tried…?"

"Daphne, to be honest I have really tried everything. You know the O'Riordan's au pair Astrid who he had a thing for? After that obsession I even offered to dress as a schoolgirl if that's what tinkled his ivories. However, when I suggested it, he looked like he was going to be sick."

"It must have been good with him once, though, surely? Back when you first met."

"Not really. Enthusiasm counts for a lot, but you'd find more passion in the keynote speech at the AGM of the Daventry Actuarial Society. He always did suffer terribly from premature… you know."

"Well, that's quite common," Daphne sympathised.

"Not in the bloody taxi on the way back from the cinema, it isn't. He's lost his deposit more often than UKIP."

Daphne's tittering could not stop Eunice, whose character assassination was in full flow.

"And as for the mechanics, well he never had a clue. Poor lamb couldn't find a clitoris if it was lit up like the Statue of Liberty on 4 July and encircled by tug boats broadcasting the Star Spangled Banner. His idea of foreplay is to tell me about his latest Hornby shunting engine, or what the P/E ratio of Vodafone shares is. I tried to get him to stimulate my 'G' spot once, and after five seconds he complained of a sprained wrist. The only time I manage to get close to climax is when I'm on top, but after two minutes he's complaining he can't breathe, and gets all red in the face. Maybe that's what actually does it for me, I don't know."

Daphne was chuckling mightily by this time.

"Still, I don't have to worry too much these days," Eunice added in a whisper. "Ever since I've got my little furry friend."

"Furry!" exclaimed Daphne. "What *are* you telling me?"

"Well, not actually furry. It's my randy little Rampant Rabbit from Ann Summers. Every time Bernard goes off to his share club on a Wednesday afternoon, I get him out of his hutch, and I get a couple of hours of real pleasure. I can highly recommend it."

"Oh, I don't know if I could. It seems so, well, artificial," Daphne said.

"That's how I felt for a long time. But in the end, if you've got the imagination you can roam the firmament of fantasy: George Clooney, Brad Pitt, Sean Connery..."

"Paul Newman, Robert Redford..." Daphne sighed.

"Jean-Paul Belmondo, I had a particularly good session with him. He was so...urgent. And French, of course. Until the bloody batteries went flat. I'll not buy Asda economy brand again, nearly ruined my afternoon."

"I'd like Gregory Peck, Montgomery Clift, Rock Hudson..."

"The last two were gay, dear. You can't have them, surely," Eunice said.

"I can if I want. In my fantasy they could be straight. Anyway, Montgomery was bi-sexual. I could have him on alternate days. And before he started on the drugs and things," Daphne said.

"Well, I suppose so. A fantasy's a fantasy after all. There's not too much choice in modern men, though. Spiky hair, bad breeding and not an ounce of gallantry. Instead of Cary Grant and Clark Gable we've got Bruce Willis and Alan Titchmarsh."

"True, they don't make them like that any more. Footballers, though, Eunice. I've had a thing for Vinny Jones for a long time. Especially when he was in that bank robbery film."

"Oh, you can't surely. He's so...uncouth. And violent."

"I know. He'd be ever so rough, wouldn't he?" Daphne purred. "He can fire his 'two smoking barrels' at me anytime."

"Steady on, Daphne. He's young enough to be your son."

"Eunice, I'm 61. They're all young enough to be my son, or were at the times they were famous. But in my fantasies I'm much younger too. A cross between Hayley Mills and Rita Tushingham."

"I think you've been at the Mills & Boon a bit too much, dear. Time for another coffee? Or is it too early to start on the Valpoli?"

Chapter Seventeen

Dunces With Wolves

Wednesday 4th June: Bradford & Bingley

Share club at the Ring o'Bells suffers Martin Gale bemoaning his financial situation. The only part of his IVA where he's not overstepped the line is his mortgage. Now, though, he's finished his fixed-rate deal and his bank, Bradford & Bingley, wants a lot more from him on the variable rate.

"Have you tried looking around for a better deal?" K.P. Sharma says. "There a lots of websites offering better deals."

"I've looked, but we've got a problem," Martin said. "It was a 95% mortgage when we started in 2006. But when we saw how prices were still going up in 2007, we added another fifteen grand secured loan to get Holly's people carrier. Of course, she wrote that off last August when she pulled out in front of a Ford Fiesta from Pass First Time School of Motoring. As it was on third party, fire and theft, we didn't get a bean apart from £260 scrap."

"My dad would have given you more than that," said Chantelle. "Come to me if you ever have a car to scrap."

"Thanks, I'll remember that. Anyway, so we've still got the secured loan, Holly's driving a ten-year-old Fiat rot box, and we're up to our neck. We applied to HSBC for one of their new cheap fixed-rate loans, but the valuation came in much lower than we thought. We're actually just into negative equity, and nobody wants to know for a remortgage."

"You were bloody daft getting that extra loan, then, weren't yer?" shouts Russell Traugh from the table by the jukebox. "And fancy not getting proper insurance, what a wazzock."

"Shut up Russ," Harry shouts. "Don't rub it in."

Martin's attitude to his debt is utterly curious, though. The more trouble he's in, the more he wants us to invest in speculative shares.

Kazakh mining stocks, obscure Ofex-listed software firms, beaten-down house builders. It all seems like double or quits. He even suggested that we buy shares in Barratt.

"It's really cheap. It's trading at much less than its net asset value. And look at the dividend! It's paying 37p and the price is only 140p, that's a yield of...quite a lot."

"Martin," K.P. said. "It's got two billion quid's worth of debt. It might break its banking covenants and have to go into administration. And let's face it, house price falls have barely begun. I don't believe in taking risks..."

"Ahem, Northern Rock?" muttered Harry, barely looking up from his copy of the *Racing Post*. At this point K.P. throws up his hands in disgust, and goes off to the bar to order a sandwich.

Chantelle, taking the order, is baffled. "I didn't think Hindus could eat beef and horseradish sarnies."

"Since when has any item on the Ring o'Bells' menu ever been made from anything that ever lived?" he responded.

"Fair point," she conceded. "But if Quorn or monosodium glutamate were ever to become sacred you'd be in big trouble."

Tuesday 10th June: Dunces With Wolves

Unexpected phone call at quarter past eight. Summoned by the dulcet klaxon of my beloved, I emerge dripping from the shower to be handed the cordless handset. It's K.P. Sharma in a state of some anxiety. Apparently Fairpoint, the former Debt Free Direct, has issued a major profit warning and is taking a pasting in the market. K.P. reads me out the first part of the statement, and it does seem pretty bad.

"The shares are already down at 45p from 77p yesterday. I'm trying to get a majority for an immediate sale for all 2000 of the club's holding," he says. "Mike Delaney agrees with me on it, Chantelle's not at home, Martin wants to hold and so does Harry."

"What baffles me," I say, as I trail drips across the bedroom floor. "Is how can a company specialising in dealing with debt problems get it so wrong just when half the country is up to their eyeballs in it?"

"Bernard, let's have the inquest later. Yours is the casting vote, and we've lost another 2p while you were talking!"

However, before I accede, I ask what the club paid for its biggest investment. The answer, horrifically, is 300p. While K.P. rushes off to make the sale, I muse over the fact that the club has lost over £5300 on one company. While we may not have anticipated today's profit warning, that is only going to lose us £700. The real crime is clear once I pull up the share price graph. While we've been supping Spitfire and munching pork scratchings at the Ring o'Bells in the last 12 months, we've casually lost a few pence every day on Fairpoint shares with no one motivated to do a damn thing about it. What a bunch of investment dunces we are, perfect fodder for the wolves of the wider financial markets.

Wednesday 11th June: Barratt Barracking

Tense times at the share club meeting. Martin Gale, having advocated Barratt shares at 140p, is now gagging with bargain-hunter's lust as they plummet to 50p. We thought he had no money left to invest, as no doubt did his IVA creditors, but apparently he's got a spread-betting account and just placed a £10 per penny up bet at 52p, hoping for the shares to recover.

"Are you out of your mind?" says Chantelle. "You can't afford to lose that kind of money can you? If it goes bankrupt you'll lose at least £500."

Martin ignores her. Staring over K.P. Sharma's shoulder at the price screen on his laptop, he only has eyes for the blue of the rising price. He's cheering it on as if it was Desert Orchid in the Two Thousand Guineas. He seems to have forgotten that Barratt isn't a gambling chip, but an employer of thousands, and a vital part of government plans to build millions of affordable homes.

Not that I can talk. My mobile rings, and it's my own spread-bet broker. My short-selling position on Rentokil is still losing money, and I'll have to stump up more margin to keep my position open. I reluctantly agree to close the position, with a loss of £108.

Close of play: While I lost money, Martin made over £200 when Barratt closed at 75p. He's cock-a-hoop, but I just fear this one success will spur him to make more such bets which cannot afford to go wrong.

Friday 13th June: Irish Stew

Had to have a good chuckle over the news this morning. The Irish have stuck two fingers up to the new EU constitution, a.k.a the Lisbon treaty. The Eurocrats, in typical high-handed fashion, refuse to concede the process is dead even though the rules require unanimity. "How could they?" they seem to be saying. "The greatest beneficiaries in the EU's history, biting the hand that fed them." What these officials don't understand is that anyone who is repeatedly lectured that something is good for them, especially if they don't understand it, is going to get bloody-minded.

Speaking of which, Eunice switched my usual breakfast of Frank Cooper's marmalade and toast for half a grapefruit, dotted with nuts and other cereal-like sweepings. I didn't even get a referendum vote.

"What's this?" I asked, prodding the offending item with a teaspoon, and getting a jet of juice in the eye.

"We talked about this, Bernard, don't you remember? When your last cholesterol test was too high, you agreed that you'd try a change of diet. Remember the saying: no to saturates, yes to polyunsaturates and monosaturates."

"I haven't the faintest idea what you're on about. Can't a poor man have a slice of toast and marmalade in peace?"

"If you want to rest in peace, certainly. This and your other meals help prolong active life," she said.

"No doubt it will give me a glossy coat and a cold wet nose too!" I retorted. "Well, I'm not a bloody dog. And I'm not eating it."

"But it's for your own good!" Eunice said gently.

"Look. I don't want a long life, because I can't afford one. I want a short life, lived the way I want, without lectures."

Saturday 14th June: Soft, Long And Very Strong

Escaped from the dietary madhouse of Endsleigh Gardens to spend the morning with my mother. Of course, in terms of lunacy that's like jumping from a lukewarm frying pan into the steel furnaces of Lakshmi Mittal. The daft bat is continuing to hoard groceries in fear of inflation, the Luftwaffe and something I hadn't even considered, a one-party state run by Alastair Darling. She's built a Wendy house entirely out of 12-packs of Andrex in the back bedroom, and is now living inside, with a sleeping bag, a gas mask, her old wireless, and seventeen out-of-date chocolate button Easter eggs. I also spied a battered tin of Minced Morsels.

"What's this for Mum?" I say, pointing at the 1970s dog food. "Is Clement Freud coming to tea?"

"Pardon?" she says. "No, I'll need that in case they use bloodhounds to try to find me. They won't attack if I feed them."

"Who's looking for you?" I ask, in wonderment at the new paranoia that is compounding her other confusions.

"Alastair Darling. He knows I didn't vote for him. I voted for the other one. His war veterans are attacking everyone, and pinching their farms, it said so on the telly. Well, every time I hear the jangle of medals I look over me shoulder and I'm giving the British Legion a very wide berth at the moment, I can tell you."

I just gape at her for a moment, until the penny drops. "Dot, that isn't about Britain or Alastair Darling. It's Zimbabwe and Robert Mugabe. You're quite safe from them in Isleworth."

Monday 15th June: Default Spreads

What a miserable start to the day. Pouring with rain from the off. Hermès screams to be let in before 6am, and I prepare to wipe her paws. She abhors having this done, and usually tries to scratch me, or at the very least hiss. This time she takes one look at the moggy towel, and races upstairs. Just as I expected, I find her sprawled next to her sleeping mistress on the £79.99 swan-patterned Egyptian cotton bedspread we bought from Debenhams two days ago. She has left an elaborate trail of filthy paw marks all over it, and now lies on her side, blinking lazily at me and yawning as if to say: "When the tyrant queen awakes it is you and not I who will be blamed for this. For I am feline royalty, to be pampered and petted. You are a mere serf in my court."

Eunice is deep in the land of nod, making a noise like a gargling wolverine. I consider the possibility of trying to ease the bedspread from beneath the cat and my wife's outstretched hand for some pre-emptive laundering. If those stains dry and can't be shifted, I know what will happen. I just can't afford to give Eunice an excuse to buy yet more linen, even if it is to help one of private equity's greatest buyout failures. If Debenhams doesn't own its own stores and is up to its eyeballs in debt, I don't want the Jones family to be involved in a bailout.

Gently, I roll up all the spare material from the bottom of the bed. The cat eyes me suspiciously, and her ears prick up as the bedspread slides around her. Finally, she digs in her claws, stopping all movement. Eunice smacks her lips and rolls over, flinging a mottled arm, with its incipient bingo-wing, over the bedspread. Without heavy lifting gear, all is lost. I grimace at the cat, which yawns dismissively at me. Yes, we both know I am for it.

For solace I pad into Lemon Curdistan and watch as the stock market opens. This is truly depressing. Prices of almost everything I own are down. Even the DotCom fund with my mother is making heavy weather of the current malaise, with Billiton and BG Group both below my purchase price. The nearest to a buoyant stock I own is Domino's Pizza. Oh well, small mercies.

I wander into the kitchen and put on the kettle. On a whim I have a quick peek in Eunice's purse. Well, it's never that quick. You could actually run two hour guided double-decker bus tours around the thing, with explanatory notes in every European language, and still not have seen all the evidence of spending contained therein. However, I do find the Debenhams store card. I then contrive to 'accidentally lose it', snipping it into fifty pieces, insert it into an empty Yakult yoghurt pot and drop it into the recycling bin. With the rate they charge on purchases, that act is probably my best investment in months.

Friday 20th June: Gates Departure

So Bill Gates is stepping down from Microsoft to spend more time with his charitable activities. His objective wasn't just to put a personal computer on every desktop. It was to make us dependent upon the damn thing, and drive us slowly mad with its irritating demands. For example, my own computer has spent the last three days demanding that I download it some security updates. Bugger off, was my reply, do it in your own time. But it kept on, and on, and on, with a pester power that most tots can't match. Throwing up insistent 'dialogue boxes' with choices that would confound Einstein. "The system has encountered a problem. Would you like to close it down immediately and lose every piece of data you have ever inputted? Or would you like to do so tomorrow, with the same result? Or would you prefer to let every cyber-criminal in the former Soviet Union pillage your online banking details?" I chose the fourth alternative. I unplugged the damn thing. I wonder if Gates himself ever had these problems?

 Elevenses: Sought solace in the Hornby drawer and discovered my eccles cakes had been removed. In their place was one of those awful green corduroy hand grenades.

"What's this, then?" I said, taking the offending item out to the Oberkitchenführer. "Where are my cakes?"

"A kiwi is far better for you," Eunice said flatly. "I put those dreadful sugary heart-stoppers out for the birds."

"Sod that," I yelled, and ran into the garden where five sparrows, two blackbirds and a one-eyed crow were squawking on the bird table. In its last moment before take-off, the carrion thief snatched the last half eccles cake in its beak, and fled to the ridge of the O'Riordan's conservatory. Safely away from me, it cawed in triumph as it gobbled the last of my elevenses. Furious beyond words, I picked up a ceramic garden pixie which some addled aunt bought Eunice in the 1980s, and hurled it at the crow. The crash of glass and some O'Riordan swearing suddenly made me realise something profound. In one creative burst of energy I'd achieved a number of long-term objectives. I'd frightened a crow, got rid of a piece of hideous kitsch and enraged our selfish neighbours.

Chapter Eighteen

Fingers In The Drawer

Tuesday 1st July: Tanfield Plunge

How glad I am that I sold my shares in Tanfield last year, when they were at 120p. I may have missed out at the 200p top (and got lectured by Perfect Peter for not seeing that the trend was my friend) but at least I made a good profit. If I'd stayed with the company after this, relatively mild, profit warning, I'd have lost it all. An 83% fall in one day seems a bit harsh, considering the company has no debt. The company is making more money now than it was when I sold, but supposedly only worth 5p a share. Perhaps it is worth a gamble?

 Elevenses: This possibility consumes my thoughts as I gobble a fresh cream slice in the den. Unfortunately, I am caught in a surprise raid on Lemon Curdistan by Special Branch (Confectionary Division). While I try to stuff the evidence back into the Hornby drawer, Eunice leans with surprising speed against the desk, slamming shut the drawer with my fingers trapped agonisingly within.

"Aaargghhh! You're amputating them, you witch!"

"Then we can pretend we're in Saudi Arabia, Bernard, can't we?" she said, only releasing them after a good ten seconds.

"I'll never type again," I moaned, holding up my throbbing digits. "Look at them, just look."

"You'll live," she said. "Besides, if I had amputated them you have a good career in shorthand, wouldn't you?" she tittered. Inside the drawer she found the remains of the fresh cream slice. "Well, well, well. A cardiac arrest in every bite," she said, prodding the item with a suspicious digit.

"Look, there's a strawberry slice in it. And a slice of kiwi. That's one of my five a day."

"You never give up, do you Bernard?" she said. "Never."

Wednesday 2nd July: K.P.'s Gamble

Everyone at share club is feeling utterly miserable at share markets that just seem to fall day after day, week after week. However, K.P. Sharma is convinced that we are due a rally.

"You've been saying that for weeks," says Harry Staines. "It's the middle of the summer, and all the toffs are at Henley or Wimbledon. What makes you think that the markets will bounce? Is that the same insight that brought us that incredible bargain Northern Rock?"

K.P. looks heavenwards. "Are you never going to let go of that, Harry? Don't you remember all the market knowledge I have brought to this club? Not to mention the use of my laptop."

"That's true," says Martin Gale. "You're being a bit harsh."

"Anyway," says K.P. "Look at these charts. The FTSE 100, and indeed the S&P 500 have bounced off key chart support levels. The stochastics are oversold, and after so many sequential falls prices are due a week or two's rebound."

"Okay Mystic Meg, what's in your crystal ball say about the 4.20pm at Kempton Park? Will it be the favourite, Downtown Boy or should I go with the 50-1 outsider Just Three Legs?" Harry asked.

"This isn't clairvoyance, it's about common sense. If buyers came in when the FTSE 100 was at about 5450 on two previous occasions, why won't they now?"

"Because everything is worse now," said Chantelle. "House prices are down, no-one can get a mortgage, and the interest rate weapon is paralysed by inflation. Even my dad's noticed some falling off in scrap metal demand."

"That may be true, but that expectation was already tied up in prices when we hit this low last time too," K.P. said. "Anyway, I'm going to be putting my money where my mouth is by buying into the HBOS rights issue."

"Here we go," said Harry. "Northern Rock II: Just when you thought it was safe to trust a bank again."

"No, Harry," K.P. said. "I'm entitled to about 1500 new shares in the rights issue with my existing holding..."

"Which you must have lost a packet on," Harry retorted.

"Yes, yes. But these shares are trading in nil paid form now. They're just tickets of entitlement to a 275p share. If the value of HBOS shares rises, which I think they will, then the nil-paid shares will soar much faster. They're only trading at 7.5p."

"Hang on a minute," I said, looking through the *FT*. "The HBOS ordinary shares closed last night at 269p, which is below the price you have to stump up for the new ones. That means the nil paid shares are worthless."

"Ah, they may be intrinsically worthless, but they do have time value. Like a warrant or call option," K.P. said. The rest of us looked around in disbelief, and however many times he tried to explain it, we were still baffled.

Thursday 3rd July: Sparks At Marks

Excellent breakfast, reading about Marks & Spencer's disappointing sales figures. I've always thought St Michael over-priced and the quality over-hyped. If I'd timed my attempts at short-selling the shares a little better I'd have made a bit of cash too.

"You seem cheerful, Bernard." Eunice says, holding down the

Telegraph so she can see me over the breakfast table. "Has Alastair Darling introduced tax breaks for model railways?"

"Unfortunately, no. Sir Stuart Rose is getting a good pasting. He saw off a 400p bid offer from Philip Green exactly four years ago, and now the shares are down at 250p. Shareholders must be kicking themselves for not getting the BHS makeover."

"Oh no, Bernard. British Home Stores is such a dreary store. Besides, I don't like that Green fellow. He looks so common."

"Ah yes, just a common billionaire," I replied.

"Well, it's common if you're that rich to go and live in a tax haven like Monaco."

"Common obviously means sensible then. If I had a billion pounds, I'd live in Antarctica if it meant Gordon Brown couldn't get his paws on it."

"Well judging by the state of those BHS slippers you'd not last ten minutes. There's a hole in the toe and you'd get frostbite. At least with M&S goods you can rely on quality and service."

"Nonsense. They wouldn't take back that bloody three-pack of tartan boxer shorts, would they?"

"Bernard, you'd worn them! No-one exchanges worn underwear, not even Primark."

"I didn't wear them, I merely tried them on."

"Bernard you're always trying it on. I'll never forget that time you tried to take back a four-year old pair of faded orange pyjamas to M&S because the elastic had gone."

"The Sale of Goods Act 1979 says..."

"Never mind that! It's when you made your point by putting on the trousers in the middle of shop to demonstrate to the sales girl that they wouldn't stay up. I've never been so embarrassed."

"It worked though, didn't it?"

"Well, it was worth giving you a full refund to get you out of the store. You looked like an escapee from Guantanamo Bay."

Friday 4th July: Random Dog Walk

Jemima and soppy boyfriend Toby have gone away for a long weekend and left me in charge of their overactive year-old black labrador, Nasdaq. As usual, this arrangement was made with about four minutes notice. Still, the hound is a great pleasure. I got him skidding about chasing a ball on the conservatory floor, and then had an idea. I'd read some years ago, in the *Wall Street Journal*, that a team of monkeys throwing darts could make better stock selections than a bunch of professionals. I just wonder if Nasdog, as I've started to call him, could do the same for me. The trouble is that Nasdog can't throw darts. I took some back copies of the *Financial Times*, laid down the share price pages right across the conservatory floor and tried to work out how we could make this work. I've got about two thousand pounds, and with the market this weak there must be some bargains to have. Perhaps Nasdog can help me find them. I started by throwing a ping pong ball onto the papers and trying to get him to fetch it. Unfortunately, in his over-enthusiasm he skidded across the floor, ripped several sheets to shreds and finally chewed the ball to pieces.

Next I screwed up a sheet of the paper and threw it across the conservatory for Nasdog to fetch. I was hoping for a clean bite mark on a particular share, but only got a very soggy mass of heavily chewed paper. I might have been baffled, but Nasdog was having a great time, watching me screwing up sheets of paper, his tail going like a windscreen wiper in a monsoon.

The front door's click announced Eunice's return from a hard day's supermarket pillage. A quick glance at the vast soggy mess of newspaper spread across the floor brought terror to my throat. Nasdog was all for greeting, but I preferred ambush. I snatched the dog and dived behind the sofa with a hand over his jaws.

We heard the click, click of slow but authoritarian heels as Eunice paced across the hardwood floor, muttering to herself about the mess. Nasdog, whining and wriggling, could barely be restrained and Eunice soon found us.

"Bernard, what are you doing down there?" she said.

"I'm training the dog."

"But he already knows how to make a mess. What are you attempting to teach him?"

"I'm going to make him a great investor. Better than Buffett. Together, we're going to beat the market."

Sunday 6th July: New Balls, Please

This is the time of year when Eunice likes to invite vegan pal Irmgard and wheelie bin-fixated neighbour Daphne Hanson-Hart over to watch television. They plan to drool over two taciturn hairy-legged Europeans smashing tennis balls at each other. Leaving them in a strawberry and Pimms-fuelled orgy of thwock (ooh!) and thwock (aah!) I walk Nasdaq the dog, or Nasdog, along deserted streets. From under a hedge he finds an old tennis ball, and after a ten minute game of 'fetch' in the park I suddenly have an idea.

On our return, I tiptoe around the ogling cronies and take Nasdog through to the garden. There in the shed I find 15 faded and shrunken tennis balls, mostly from the days when I attempted to chivvy a 13-year-old Jemima out of the house and away from an unhealthy interest in popular crooning groups. That of course failed as soon as I pulled a muscle in my back, which was about fifteen minutes into our first practice.

Now though, these balls have a use in my attempt to recreate the monkey-and-darts random share picking experiment. If I just write the name of a market sector on each ball, and throw them from a bucket down the garden I will be able to get Nasdog to retrieve one. It takes a good half hour to mark them up using a felt-tip, all the while watched by the slobbering and over-excited dog. I'm just about ready, when Eunice emerges from the conservatory.

"Bernard, it's your mother on the phone. She says her television's stuck on CBeebies but she wants to watch Rod Laver and Billie-Jean…"

"Oh God. I've told her time and again to change channels with the remote, and not to touch the connections on the back. She'll electrocute herself."

"Look. Can you come and talk to her? She's driving me barmy. And Nadal's got two set points. Oh, and would you put the kettle on when you come in? And look, Nasdog's done something."

So I stopped what I was doing, went inside, spoke to my loopy mother and made the tea. Later, I would clear up after Jem's dog. What a life. Come on, Bernard, are you really to spend the rest of it at the beck and call of women? Almost certainly, yes.

Monday 7th July: Consumer Electronics 1955-Style

Spent an infuriating day round at my mother's. She complained she missed the tennis because the TV set blew up.

"I want a British TV next time. This Japanese stuff is rubbish," Dot said, looking at her ten-year-old Sony. All attempts to convey the importance of Japanese just-in-time manufacturing, a superior industrial ethos and the technological dominance of this sophisticated nation were lost on my mother. To her the Japanese were still building railways across Burma using PoW labour, and trying to take India from our Empire. Perhaps that is why she stabbed the television.

"No TV is going to be happy about having a screwdriver jammed into the air vent. You've got to stop doing things like that," I said, inspecting the partially melted back cover of the tube.

"I was trying to change the channel."

"Mum, if I've told you once I've told you a thousand times, you've got to use the remote. You can't change channel like you used to on a 1955 Bush."

"But it doesn't work, Bernard. Look." She pointed the remote at the screen and pressed several buttons randomly.

"It's not going to work now because the TV's broken, isn't it? Besides, you're holding the remote control back to front," I said.

"But how can I tell? It looks the same both ways."

"No it doesn't, Mum, hold it so that the writing's the right way up. Look." I showed her how to hold the device.

She took it from me and pressed several buttons. "Well, it doesn't work any better your way round."

"Of course it doesn't now! That's because the bloody TV's broken. As I just told you, you stupid woman!"

"Bernard, there's no need to swear. If you'd not lost your temper, you wouldn't have broken it, now would you?"

At this point I really did lose my temper and kicked the TV hard, at which point it fell off its stand and onto me.

Close of play: Waiting in A&E to have my foot bandaged. The fellow next to me is reading the evening paper which shows FTSE around 5400. One of those chartist chappies said we might get a bounce here. I do hope so. I'm down 23% this year, and have hardly any cash left to buy bargains.

Tuesday 8th July: Choosing A Dog Stock

With Eunice out shopping (again) I return to my task with Nasdog. I fill the bucket with marked tennis balls and hurl them down the garden as far as I can. Nasdog leaps after them and jumps into and out of bushes before finally returning with one. Will it be banks? Construction or property? However, the damn dog now seems to be a little possessive of his chosen ball, and doesn't want to let me have it. He thinks it is more fun to pretend to drop it, but change his mind at the last minute and have me chase him.

Finally, I get a grip on the saliva-covered object and gently extricate it from his growling mouth. What's written on it? Slazenger, and nothing else. On closer inspection, this isn't one of my balls anyway. Probably one of the bloody O'Riordan's. So I pretend to throw it back in the bushes, and the dog falls for it, sprinting back like a great black rubbery bundle to the bottom of the garden. This time he does retrieve one of my balls. The sector is chemicals. Well, that's a bit uninspiring. I repeat the task of labelling the balls, but this time with each carrying the name of a stock within the chemical sector.

What does Nasdog bring back? Zotefoams. I'd never even heard of it. I look the firm up on its website: 'A world leader in cross-linked block foams.' I'm none the wiser, quite honestly. Now I'm in a bit of a quandary. I've got £2000 to invest, but I'm not sure that Zotefoams is really going to set the stock market firmament ablaze. A bit of research shows that it has a market cap of less than £30 million, and a lowish P/E of under 10. The shares have been falling all year, but there is a 6% dividend yield and little debt. Still, if this year in the stock market has taught me one thing, it is that my own judgment has not beaten the market. Perhaps the dog's judgment will serve me better. So I go online, and spend my hard-earned cash on Zotefoams shares at 82p.

Wednesday 9th July: Insider Tip

K.P. Sharma is looking a little glum as the rest of us arrive for share club. Harry immediately starts needling him, a tactic that he has down to a fine art.

"How are those lovely HBOS nil paid shares doing, then?" he asks. "Have you doubled your money yet?"

"No," K.P. replied "I sold yesterday at a 40% loss when it was clear that there was not going to be a bounce."

"That kind of thing is all very speculative, isn't it?" said Martin Gale, a pot never too proud to call the kettle black. "I've got a real bargain. I borrowed some more money from my sister and bought three thousand shares in Persimmon at 217p. Her lodger's sister in law's boyfriend works for them as a plasterer, or did until they made him redundant in 2006. He says they are really cheap."

"Another quality insider tip from boardroom sources," murmured Chantelle, as she dried glasses behind the bar.

Thursday 10th July: Blazing Comet

Drove back to Dot's yet again, to take her to buy a new television. We arrive at the local Comet warehouse, where every wall is lined with gigantic TV screens. The only snag is that every single one is tuned to the same channel. It is presumably a David

Attenborough programme, because shambling across the screen is an androgynous giggling yeti, apparently dressed by Oxfam.

"What on earth is it?" Dot asks.

"That's Russell Brand," the assistant explains.

"Oh. Same make as my old kettle," she nods. "They have branched out, haven't they? I knew they did toasters."

"No Mum, you're thinking of Russell Hobbs," I say, asking the assistant if we could find a different channel. Eventually we got my mother down away from the 40" widescreen monsters to something in keeping with her style.

"These are all plastic, though," Dot complains. "Don't they have one in wood? My first telly was made of wood. And it only cost thirty guineas. I mean, look at the price of these!"

"It also only had a ten inch screen, and the sound was as crackly as a reverse-charge call from New Guinea," I say.

"Well, I'll only buy a British one," she says.

The assistant looked dubious, but consults a manager who comes over. There had used to be several TV plants in Wales, he says, but most of the work had now gone to Eastern Europe. The JVC plant in Scotland and the Philips plant in the North East had closed too, he admits. "What about Belgium? We've got a portable TV made in Belgium. Would that do?" he asks.

Eventually we settled on a robust-looking flat-screen Panasonic for £200, made in Taiwan. Dot agrees only after I whisper in her ear that it's actually pronounced Daiwan, and is a new eco town in mid-Wales.

Sunday 13th July: All Creatures Grate And Smell

Today should have been a Friday 13th. Heavy, overcast weather and a grim sense of foreboding. Worse was to come. Toaster conks out at breakfast, so forced to use the grill. Burned four slices of bread (distracted reading *Chronic Investor* magazine) before finally getting to the last pair before immolation set in. After request from the Windolene Witch, I look again at her washing machine, which leaks more often than MI5. Can't find anything wrong with it, but when Eunice tests it with a heavy load of bedclothes it makes an ominous grinding sound and now it won't work at all. She then sent me to vacuum up my burned crumbs from the kitchen floor. However, our Electrolux, which even normally has only the sucking power of an asthmatic mayfly, gave one giant slurp and died.

"What's the matter now?" said Eunice, as I started a detailed Anglo-Saxon dressing down of the blasted device.

"The damn thing's just stopped," I said.

"Oh no! Still, it wouldn't have happened, Bernard, if we'd bought a Dyson," she said. "But you're just too tight, aren't you?"

"What do you mean? These retail at nearly £200 don't they?"

"Perhaps. But this one was £130 at Somerfield, in 2006. A bargain, you said. It was on special offer because the box was crushed where it had been dropped. Don't you recall? No wonder Comet, Currys and Dixons sales are in such a state, having to cope with cheapskates like you."

"Well, it's a competitive marketplace, and the supermarkets are muscling their way in," I said, as I began to work on the cleaner's plug. "With any luck it's only the fuse."

"Not with that burning smell, Bernard. It's destined for the hoover happy hunting grounds I should think."

"That should be something for the fossil hunters to find in a millennium or two. I mean, we should get David Attenborough over here to catalogue this. With the microwave dying last week, your hair tongs, my electric razor and all this lot today, this has been the greatest mass extinction since the end of the Cretaceous period."

"Ah yes," Eunice replied. "I can see the headline: 'Life on earth to end. Humanity expires. Bernard Jones blamed. Too tight to pay for five billion-year extended warranty'. Still, I expect you're going to say it was all caused by a Comet impact."

Monday 14th July: Bastille Day Massacre

Markets dropped to the floor today faster than Marie-Antoinette's severed head. Everyone says that FTSE's going to drop below 5000 at some stage. It's a shame Peter Edgington has fallen out with us, I could do with his advice at a time like this.

 Close of Play: Market ended where it started after a failed rally attempt.

Tuesday 15th July: Worse Still

Market plunges well below 5200. I feel I should sell something, but what? Only two stocks are doing well, Compass and Domino's Pizza. Should I ditch those before they drop sharply too? Or is it better to sell losers like all the pundits say? I've had Lloyds TSB for years, but I've lost more on the share price than I ever gained from its dividends. I'm tempted to ditch it, but then I might miss out on a recovery. Even oil stocks and miners are looking weak.

Elevenses: An enormous fresh cream éclair, savoured while renovating a branch line on the railway layout in the loft. I'll ignore shares for a while, too depressing.

Wednesday 16ᵗʰ July: Share Club Deserted

HBOS shares, of which K.P. Sharma was a champion, are well below their rights issue price. Not surprisingly he doesn't turn up for share club at the Ring o'Bells. Neither does Harry Staines nor Martin Gale. Only Chantelle is here, working behind the bar.

"It's amazing, innit," she says, serving me a pint of Spitfire. "Here we are, with share prices more than 20% cheaper than a year ago, and no-one turns up at the club to discuss what bargains to buy. Yet last summer, with sky-high prices we had a full house every time."

"It just shows we don't buy shares like we buy toasters or vacuum cleaners," I said.

Russell Traugh, who overheard our conversation slides up, his nylon trousers whistling with every step. "I can get you more than 20% off a Dyson, if you're interested."

I obviously did look interested, so Russell continued. "It's reconditioned, looks good as new. Ninety quid."

Chantelle looked at us both. "Only those who never have to use a vacuum cleaner themselves would ever buy a cheap one."

"That's settled, then," I chuckled. "I'll take it."

Chapter Nineteen

Equitable Treatment

Thursday 17th July: A Kiss For Ann

Oh Joy! Finally, parliamentary ombudsperson Ann Abraham has released her Equitable Life report! She confirms that we victims have been short-changed by regulators as well as the company. Though I wasn't one of those whose annuities were over-generously guaranteed, when the courts ruled that Equitable Life did have to compensate them, it was my with-profit policy that got ransacked to pay for it. Perhaps now we will finally get some compensation. If so, that woman deserves a kiss.

 Close of play: Huge rise on Wall Street. Perhaps the market really is turning around. Feel happier than I have for some time.

Friday 18th July: Death Or Glory

Market recovering sharply today, including Zotefoams which fell from the 82p I bought it at, hit 75p and is now back unchanged. Good old Nasdog! Maybe I can get the animal to choose more stocks for me. Eunice, however, has other things on her mind.

"Look," she says, showing me the *Daily Mail*. "The government is going to spend £286 million extending consumer choice, by allowing us to choose how we want to die."

"Hmm. It might be worth that if we could choose how others would die. I'd like the Harmsworth brothers to end their days in a skip lorry reversing accident," I said.

"Health Secretary Alan Johnson didn't make any mention of skips. It's hospice or home. Still, it says you do get an emergency 24-hour team of nurses that can come round to look after you."

"Team of nurses, eh? Well, that would be a good way to go."

Eunice caught me with a basilisk glare. "Bernard, grow up. You can't cope with one woman, yet alone a team."

"It'd probably kill me. That's the point." I said cheerfully.

The stony silence that ensued reminded me to change the subject to something closer to Eunice's heart.

"I'm going to buy you a Dyson this weekend," I said.

"My goodness. That's a policy U-turn worth of Alastair Darling. Are you unwell?" she asked.

"Well, I thought it was about time to back British-owned talent and industry. James Dyson's a great entrepreneur, and even though he's moved manufacturing to Malaysia, I think we should give him a try. As you say, the quality is better than its rivals."

Eunice paused. "What a fibber. You've got a cheap one, haven't you?"

"Now why do you always think...?"

"Bernard, I know you of old."

"There's no trust in this marriage, is there?" I said.

"Alright. I'll ask no questions, but you've got to do the vacuuming for the first week. If the machine survives a week of your mishandling then I'll know it's alright."

Saturday 19th July: Fairtrade Fight

Picked up the Dyson from Russell on the way to the supermarket. Eunice has given me a list that's longer than *War and Peace* but I plan to do a little editing. I'm switching to Lidl for the basics, and cutting out Waitrose altogether. There'll be hell to pay, no doubt, but if I'm doing the shopping, it'll be my way and at half the price.

On my return, my prediction is borne out.

"Bernard, this isn't Fairtrade coffee. I stipulated Fairtrade."

"This is the same stuff, grown in the same benighted country by the same down-trodden peasants. And it's half the price."

"Bernard, you're become a jack-booted coffee fascist, oppressing the Latin American masses," Eunice said.

"What nonsense," I retorted. "Fairtrade is the just the latest fad in market segmentation. It's a way of gulling emotional housewives into buying off guilt with their food consumption."

"But Fairtrade means the farmers get the extra money."

"In which case, farmers will see the money to be made, you'll get more coffee produced, a greater glut and underlying prices will fall further. You can't repeal the laws of the market, which has always been that farmers are price takers not price makers."

"So you believe in free markets, right or wrong?"

"Of course. There's Milton Friedman and whatsisname Hayek coursing through these veins you know." I looked at the groceries spread around on the kitchen table. "So what's for dinner then?"

"Well, I thought I'd make a steak and kidney pie with roast potatoes and cauliflower, with raspberries and meringue after."

"Marvellous. That's what I call fighting food. None of this vegan rubbish. Just good solid British steak and kidney."

"Of course, there's a £10 fee for cooking services."

"What!"

"Free market, Bernard. It's barely minimum wage for the time it will take. Of course, you can always try making it yourself."

Monday 21ˢᵗ July: Vindicated On Domino's

Domino's Pizza has done me proud in its annual results. My best performing share has proved what I always thought, that when you feel like eating out but can't afford it, the next best thing is to order in for a fraction of the price. With the number of new outlets being opened, and the limited competition from nationally-known names, I think we can call this the deep-profit Bernard recipe, lots of topping but a good financial base too. The shares topped 200p for the first time in months.

Tuesday 22ⁿᵈ July: Community Service

I have a great idea for teaching young thugs and drunks a lesson. You make them repeatedly vacuum a house under Eunice's nagging supervision. This tortuous form of community service is almost as unbearable as waterboarding. After an hour and a half being told "No, not like that" or "No, no, you're missing great lumps" or "You certainly need more practice with the crevice tool" I was quite ready to admit being Osama Bin Laden's bodyguard, his driver or even his chiropodist.

Worse still is that the 'new' Dyson from Russell Traugh is utterly gutless, having been unable to get moggy fluff off the hall carpet. Its perspex bin was already half full of builder's dust and bits of wood shavings, which Russell said was where he had tested it, but I'm not so sure. First day I almost fell down the stairs when I got the flex caught around my leg, smashed it into my shins trying to get it up the loft ladder to the railway layout room, and covered myself with dust when I opened the bin-thing the wrong way. The whole process so amused Eunice that she invited Daphne Hanson-Hart in to watch. They trailed after me with mugs of coffee and ginger nuts, commenting on my progress.

Wednesday 23rd July: Dodgy Mortgage

Martin Gale is jubilant. He borrowed from his sister to buy shares in Persimmon a fortnight ago at 217p, and now they're 350p.

"Time to sell, definitely," said Mike Delaney.

"Get out while you're ahead," said Chantelle. "Especially seeing as you've borrowed the cash."

"Double-up," says Harry. "Sell the shares, put the cash into a long spread-bet on Persimmon and ride 'em to recovery."

"What an incredibly irresponsible piece of advice," said K.P. Sharma. "I can't think of anything worse..."

"Northern Rock?" retorted Harry.

While K.P and Harry descended into their usual bickering I said to Martin. "Why don't you sell half and run the rest? That's a decent way to hedge your bets."

"I like that," said Martin. "The ones I sell, I'll put the proceeds into Bradford & Bingley. They look worth a punt."

Russell Traugh, leaning at the bar, said. "You lot are crazy. You're digging around in the rubbish that's going to fall again."

"I bet you've lost money in the last year," said Harry.

"No, I'm up," he said. "Look at ASOS and Dignity."

"Didn't you have shares in Corin?" said K.P. Sharma. "They got killed didn't they?" He tapped away at his PC. "That's right. It's down from 500p to 150p after Stryker stopped ordering from it."

"Yeah, but I only had a few," Russell said.

"But you had lots of that Ukrainian farmer didn't you? I don't think they're doing well," K.P. said.

"I'm in profit from my buy price, but not this year," Russell said. "But I still think I'm way ahead of you lot."

Thursday 24ᵗʰ July: Massage In A Bottle

A whole day to myself. Eunice is going off to Tunbridge Wells all morning and by the time she gets back, I'll be off to share club.

"What was it you said you were doing?" I asked as she was about to leave.

"I'm having an Ayurvedic massage and some ear candling."

"What on earth are you on about?"

"Well I got a bit tired of the same old aromatherapy fragrances with Helen, and when I saw Irmgard last week she said that my chakras still seem a little unbalanced. She goes to Tom, who's apparently divine at rebalancing your energy centres. So it's my first session with him today."

"What a lot of New Age codswallop. You'll spend a fortune, come back smelling like a Botswanan brothel and be in too much of a trance to feel like cooking my dinner for the next three days."

"With any luck," she said brightly.

"Well," I murmured to myself after the door had slammed shut. "You'd just better check that this Tom fellow isn't a bearded Yugoslav war criminal in disguise. If it's Radovan Karadzic you'll get colonically *and* ethnically cleansed."

Friday 25ᵗʰ July: Blue-Blooded Broker Shock

Can hardly believe the *Telegraph* this morning. Malcolm Calvert, 63, of Cobham Surrey, a very distinguished looking retired director of blue-blooded brokers Cazenove has been accused of insider trading. This isn't some greasy barrow boy cum derivatives trader from the East End of which one could believe such things. There he is, looking like a retired wing commander with his four-button blazer and cuff links, fending off cameras as he leaves the court. What kind of world do we live in now? 'My word is my bond' seems long forgotten. Or perhaps I am just a little envious that in my entire career at the MoD, aiding the procurement of ordnance and equipment for our armed forces, no one ever offered me an insider tidbit with which I could feather my nest. I shall follow this case with the same energy and focus that Eunice did for the Max Mosley sadomasochistic orgy trial.

Back in Lemon Curdistan I log on to the PC and see something very irritating. Rentokil has issued another profit warning. I was forced to close out my short position on the shares several weeks ago when they stubbornly refused to fall after the last profit warning, and here they are down at 71p with a new one. Why is my timing so abysmal? I think the God of Mammon has it in for me.

 Elevenses: I notice that the Hornby drawer has again been ransacked by intruders. The last two lemon curd tarts have disappeared, and instead there is a small slice of cake. Now this is very suspicious. Eunice never leaves me cake. This object, in clingfilm on a paper plate, appears to be a little more orange than ordinary cake and there are numerous dark brown nutty bits in it. There is a kind of icing too, which appears to be good news, unless it's merely some cunningly disguised plastic explosive. I think I'll have to send a sample off to Defra first before I let it into the food chain. I hold up a small sample to Prescott, the suede covered pig. "What do you think, eh? Is it poison or not?"

Eunice walks in just as I'm having this conference.

"Aha. Talking to stuffed animals! I could have you sectioned for less."

"What is this stuff?" I say, holding up the paper plate.

"It's a present from Irmgard."

I drop the plate like it was scalding. I clearly recall how last year Eunice's left-leaning friend fell 90 degrees further than usual after eating a Tesco tahini roulade that I had bought.

"It's alright, Bernard, she has forgiven you."

I inspected the cake again. I had not realised that Irmgard's life-threatening allergy to sesame seeds would have any relevance to tahini. I still suspected the vegan harridan would be seeking revenge, in a time and a manner of her choosing. This could be it.

"It's carrot cake with fennel and jute seeds and tofu icing."

"Well, you have to hand it to her," I said. "You'd never guess. It almost looks edible."

"It IS edible. Bernard, you are so suspicious. Irmgard has cooked for some very big names you know."

"Ah yes, Alexander Litvinenko, Viktor Yuschenko, Rasputin, Snow White..."

"Bernard, it's extremely good for you. It's got a week's supply of every essential mineral..."

"Ah yes, I'm sure each slice contains 100% of the recommended daily allowance of arsenic, cadmium and dioxin."

At which point, Eunice grabbed the now rather battered cake, whipped off the cling film and ate it herself.

Saturday 26th July: Debenhams Card Missing

Eunice returns flustered from a truncated shopping trip.

"Bernard, you wouldn't have seen the Debenhams store card would you? I couldn't find it anywhere."

"Why would I know where it is? I never use it," I reply. My secret, of course, is that the said item lies in twenty pieces on council landfill somewhere as part of clandestine Jones family budget control. However, if I thought that this would curtail Eunice's retail activities I was wrong. She heaved four full carrier bags onto the kitchen table and shook her head.

"It was very embarrassing. I had to pay cash, so I confined myself to the essentials," she says.

I look through just one bag and find a new definition of essential: A cut glass olive oil drizzler (£16.99), a shape-sorter thing for measuring spaghetti portions (£6 from Le Vrai Gourmet), a granite mortar and pestle for £20, a plastic spear thing for disembowelling lemons (£2.50, and called a 'lemon reamer'.)

"Can I ask what it was you discarded as inessential?" I said.

"I didn't get a new toaster," she said.

Typical. It was the one thing we actually needed.

Chapter Twenty

Dot Goes Missing

Thursday 7ᵗʰ August: Dreams Of Yesteryear

Got a call from Dot late this evening. She was very confused and tearful and sounded like she'd been having hallucinations about my late father.

"I saw Geoffrey at the foot of the bed last night, Bernard. He said he was waiting for me."

"You probably dreamed it, Mum," I said.

"No, I'd been sitting up in bed, listening to the radio, and suddenly it went all crackly. Then I saw him, and he asked how we all were. Then he said that he was waiting for me to come to him. He asked why I'd been such a long time."

"Well, he did die in 1988, Mum. But you've been living your life, having a whale of a time, haven't you?"

"No Bernard, I haven't. I've been on my own for years and years. All there is to do is watch telly. When I go out on the street there's fewer and fewer people I know. The area's all changed, and all the old shops are gone and boarded up. Back in the old days people used to knock on your door to see how you were doing, but now there's no milkman any more and there's a different postman every day. Even Mr Khan's Post Office has closed now."

"There's the lady from Social Services, isn't there? And we come round to see you quite a lot."

"You never seem to be here when I need you."

"Well, Mum, to be fair you did refuse to move nearer us, and you repeatedly made it clear you don't want to go into a home. I don't know what more we can do for you," I said gently.

"I want to go to Geoffrey," she said. "I'm old and I'm not well."

Friday 8ᵗʰ August: Feeling Better

Full of foreboding, I drove round to Frobisher Road to see my mother. She seemed in much better spirits, and I took her out to the local Baker's Oven where we shared a family-size sausage roll, two chocolate éclairs and a pot of tea. While we were sitting there she told me that she wanted to draft a new will. I tried not to let my jaw fall open, something helped by the gluey consistency of the sausage roll. However, I couldn't avoid a gasp of flaky pastry crumbs which showered into my cup of tea.

"You see, Bernard, I have got a bit of money as you know. Mary Asterby of the WI says that I should probably not have all this money in shares at this stage in my life, especially with prices going down. She thinks I should do some estate planning to avoid inheritance taxes."

"That's good advice, if a bit late. It's advice I tried to give you for many years you know," I said, barely able to believe my luck.

She then said she had arranged to see her solicitor next Monday. I look forward to getting my own back on the smug and pompous Herbert Ridley of Ridley, Gryp and Poultice, who last time we spoke refused to even disclose what the current state of my mother's will was.

Saturday 9ᵗʰ August: Bad Omens

I woke up today in a good humour, highly encouraged by my mother's recent burst of good sense and lucidity. However, matters quickly took a decided turn for the worse. At noon I tried to ring her, my normal time to do so, hoping to finalise arrangements for next week. There was no reply. She's never been able to work the answer machine that I gave her, so I kept trying to ring on and off for the next three hours. A little bit concerned, I rang Mrs Harrison, one of her near neighbours who went to investigate for me. I waited for a few minutes until her breathless return. Mrs Harrison had with her a note which had been taped to Dot's door. It simply said: 'Gone to meet Geoffrey. Shan't be coming back.'

I almost fainted at that shock, but retained enough composure to ask Mrs Harrison if she could see any sign of Maurice the mobility vehicle in the vestibule. No, it wasn't there. She knocked for several minutes, without getting a reply, and then under my instruction used the spare back door key which Dot always kept under the cast-iron Andrew Lloyd-Webber boot scraper. A few minutes later she rang me on Dot's phone to say there was no sign of her, but that the house looked unusually tidy. She also noticed that Dot's best overcoat and headscarf were not in their normal place on the coat rack. As soon as I got off the phone, I heard Eunice's keys at the door. She took one look at my face and knew something was wrong.

"My mother's run away to meet my father!"

"But he died in the 1980s," Eunice said. "Silly old thing."

"No, Eunice, she's really gone. I had Mrs Harrison look around the house. Maurice isn't there, so she's off somewhere. She's got her best clothes."

"Well, start with the police," Eunice said.

However, after dialling 999 and getting through to the incident room I was lectured in no uncertain terms by the female duty officer that this was not an emergency.

"But she's 92 years old!"

"Yes, but you say she's only been missing for two hours. If she's capable of using a mobility scooter she must have some common sense," the WPC said. "We can't file a missing person's report yet, but we'll see if we have a Community Support Officer in the area to keep an eye out for her."

There was no way out of it, we'd have to go around to look for the daft old bat ourselves. Reluctantly, Eunice agreed to cancel her Ayurvedic massage with Tom and come with me round to Isleworth to look for her. Despite my great haste, we soon got stuck in slow moving traffic on the M25.

"So where could she have gone?" Eunice said.

"Well, Dad's buried at Hanwell cemetery, so we'll start there. Apart from that I don't have much of a clue."

"Do you think she could get Maurice all that way?" she said.

"If she remembered to charge him up. However, I recall her trying to find somewhere to pour old chip oil into the battery compartment, having seen on TV that you can run tractors on it."

"I suppose that's encouraging under the circumstances. I think we should start from her house, and follow the route she would have to have taken."

"Assuming she's going to the cemetery," I said.

Our first stop was at Mrs Harrison's, who said Dot had not returned. Letting myself into Dot's house, I phoned every number on her emergency contact list. That included all the social service organisations, the old folks away-day groups and the community centre. I even phoned Mary Asterby of the WI to see if Dot was there. No luck.

We then drove to the cemetery, passing from the noise of the Uxbridge Road to the quiet beyond the mock-gothic arch. There was almost no one around. We took a while to locate my father's grave, which was further back than I recalled. The fact that I couldn't remember exactly where it was filled me with guilt. The black glossy granite headstone, with its simple inscription and its space for Dot, still looked relatively new. The same could not be said for the flowers in the vase beneath which had wilted away years ago. There was no evidence that anyone had visited the grave recently. Certainly I hadn't been for many years.

Baffled how to continue, we then drove back to Dot's house. Eunice picked through the family photographs, asking questions about where Dot and Geoffrey got married, where they went on honeymoon and where they were happiest. "I mean if she's gone to meet him, she'd probably choose somewhere were they were very happy together, wouldn't she?"

"That's a brilliant idea," I said. "Unfortunately I can't recall too many details, not having been alive at the time."

"Come on, Bernard, she must have told you."

"They were married in Ripon, so she wouldn't be able to get there easily. The honeymoon was on the Isle of Man, if I remember rightly. But as for where they were happiest, I really don't know."

By six o'clock we were getting peckish, so decided to go in search of a pizza or curry. We walked the same route, out of Frobisher Road and up Twickenham Road towards Hanwell, that Dot might have taken. Despite the roar of traffic, there seemed a warm, pleasant light and a sweet but pungent aroma. The latter I put that down to the fact that we were just over a hundred yards away from the giant West Middlesex Drainage Works.

Just before Isleworth railway station we passed an overgrown embankment leading down to a culvert, choked with supermarket trolleys and litter. Something down there drew my eye. Amongst the rubbish, I could see an upended red mobility vehicle. When I pointed it out to Eunice she put a hand over her mouth. Gingerly, I made my way through the broken and rusted railings and descended ten feet on a slippery track. I righted the vehicle and inspected it. It was the same make and model as my mother's, though the plastic panelling had been smashed on the left-hand side. On the steering column was a decisive identification mark: a plastic badge bought for Dot by Jem, bearing the slogan 'Hell's Grannies'. This was Maurice all right, but where was Dot? My heart was hammering as I poked through the dock weeds and ragwort that grew all around the culvert. For all my machinations about getting my hands on Dot's inheritance, I realised that I would give it all up forever, just to know that she was safe and alive.

Beyond the coke bottles, the odd syringe, dog excrement and broken glass there was nothing. The odd thing was that the vehicle could never have been driven down here at all, and Dot would never have been strong enough to push it. Something happened here, involving someone else other than Dot. I had no idea what, but it didn't look good.

"Do you think your mother might have caught a train to London?" Eunice said.

"It's possible."

"If she'd left Maurice at the station, it might have been hooligans who tossed it down here after she'd gone."

"That's the most optimistic scenario I can think of," I said.

We walked up to Isleworth Station, hoping to find some platform staff who might have remembered Dot passing through today. Though the ticket office was manned, the fellow there said he'd only come on duty half an hour before. There seemed no one else to ask. The platforms above, which spanned St John's Road, had just a scattering of travellers. They were all on the north side, the line heading into Waterloo. The other platform was deserted. I crossed to it, and saw that anyone standing here would have had an excellent view of whatever happened to Maurice, and possibly to Dot, at the embankment.

Something at the edge of recollection was nudging me about why my mother may have gone to London. There was a rhyme that Dad used to sing to me and Yvonne when we were children:

'A wonderful bird is the pelican,

His beak can hold more than his belly can.'

There was something about that rhyme that meant something to them as a couple. Something related to how they met. Suddenly I realised.

"Come on, Eunice, let's get dinner up in town. I think that's where we might find my mother."

So we took the train to Waterloo and changed for the Northern Line on the underground where we mingled with the pre-theatre crowds. However, at Charing Cross we emerged and crossed Trafalgar Square. Overhead enormous flocks of pigeons were wheeling overhead, changing from grey to white as they turned in the dying light.

"Come on, we've got to hurry I said," as I steered my baffled wife through numerous underpasses and not a few Pelican crossings. We walked down the Mall, and took an immediate left turn into Horse Guards Road. To the left, beyond Horse Guards Parade and the imperial statues of Clive, Kitchener and Mountbatten were the great institutions of contemporary power: Downing Street, the Treasury and the Foreign & Commonwealth Office. To the right, was a magnet of a different and more emotional sort. There was St James's Park, looking golden and peaceful in the gathering dusk, with a slight mist gathering over the lake. The cackle of ducks and the cawing of crows drowned out the distant roar of traffic. Couples sat close on benches, while breathless joggers did their early evening turns around the paths, iPods strapped to their waists. In the centre, on Duck Island, a solitary pelican could be seen, spreading its wings.

"We've come a long way, Bernard, I do hope you're right," said Eunice.

"I'm pretty certain this is where she'll be." My recollections had gradually crystallised around a story that my mother told me many times when I was young. That on 20 July 1936, in the full flush of her youth, she had taken a long lunchtime break from the offices in Pall Mall to sit in St James's Park. While she was there a young gentleman had walked past, and tipped his hat at her. A few minutes later he walked back, tipped his hat again, and then sat at the other end of the bench. Nothing was said for a while, but as my mother ate a sandwich a pelican wandered out from the lake and walked right up to the bench. My mother took a corner of the sandwich, and tossed it to the bird. Thus emboldened, the bird walked right up and took the rest, right out of my mother's hands. "So much for lunch", was what she said to the gentleman, as he chased the bird away.

"He was ever so polite," was what Dot had always said. "He said 'I hope it would not be too forward if I were to offer to replace the meal you have lost, in my company?'"

So off they went to a Lyons Corner House for tea, even though my mother risked trouble for being late back at work. I retold the story to Eunice as we walked around the lake, carefully looking at each bench in turn. Fifty yards ahead, close to the Blue Bridge which spans the lake at its narrowest part, I saw my mother. In her best coat with her headscarf on and her hands resting on an umbrella, I could still imagine the scene 72 years ago which had inspired this act of remembrance, and in her slight figure I could even see the elegant and innocent young woman who was so affected by it.

My mother didn't look up as I approached, but she didn't seem surprised we had found her.

"Hello, Mum," I said, sitting on the bench next to her.

"Hello, Bernard."

"We've been on a wild pelican chase to find you, you know. We've all been very worried."

"I've been here since ten o'clock this morning, waiting. He's not turned up like he said he would."

"That's men for you," muttered Eunice under her breath.

"Mum," I said. "It's getting a bit chilly now. I think we'd better leave it for today, don't you?"

She nodded and let me help her up, as frail as a bird under the thick wool of her coat.

"Come on, let's get you a nice cup of tea. Then we can take you home with us. I think that's what Geoffrey would have wanted, don't you?"